This Is Not Normal

This Is Not Normal

The Collapse of Liberal Britain

William Davies

VERSO

London • New York

To my mum

First published by Verso 2020
© William Davies 2020

The chapters in this book draw on the following publications: Chapter 1: 'Initial Ruptures', Political Economy Research Centre (24 June 2016); 'What Sort of Crisis Is This?', openDemocracy (30 June 2016); 'The Crisis of Statistical Fact', see 'How statistics lost their power – and why we should fear what comes next', *Guardian* (19 January 2017); 'Strong and Stable' see 'Theresa May's vapid vision for a one-party state', *New York Times* (11 May 2017). Chapter 2: 'The Corbyn Shock' see 'Reasons for Corbyn', *London Review of Books* (13 July 2017); 'The Riddle of Tory Brexitism' see 'What are they after?', *London Review of Books* (8 March 2018); 'The Revenge of Sovereignty on Government' see 'Boris Johnson, Donald Trump and the Rise of Radical Incompetence', *New York Times* (13 July 2018); 'The Lure of Exit' see 'Leave, and leave again', *London Review of Books* (7 February 2019); 'The Demise of Liberal Elites' see 'Why we stopped trusting elites', *Guardian* (29 November 2019); 'Comedy or Demagoguery' see 'The funny side of politics', openDemocracy (9 April 2019). Chapter 3: 'Democracy without Representation' see 'They don't even need ideas', *London Review of Books* (20 June 2019); 'The Conservative Selectorate' see 'A fanatical sect has hijacked British politics', *New York Times* (25 June 2019); 'England's New Rentier Alliance', Political Economy Research Centre (1 August 2019); 'The Johnson Press' see 'How the Johnson campaign is bringing Trump's media tactics to Britain', openDemocracy (13 June 2019); 'The Blizzard of Lies' see 'Reasons to be cheerful', *London Review of Books* (18 July 2019); 'Why Everyone Hates the "Mainstream Media"' see 'Why can't we agree on what's true any more?', *Guardian* (19 September 2019); 'Mutations of Leadership' see 'How to be prime minister', *London Review of Books* (26 September 2019); 'The Party of Resentment' see 'The Tories have lost their ideology. Now they are merely the party of resentment', *Guardian* (1 October 2019); 'The Berlusconification of Britain' see 'How Boris Johnson and Brexit are Berlusconifying Britain', *Guardian* (4 December 2019); 'The Johnson Victory' see 'For Johnson's Tories, the collapse of public trust isn't a problem – it's an opportunity', *Guardian* (13 December 2019).

1 3 5 7 9 10 8 6 4 2

Verso
UK: 6 Meard Street, London W1F 0EG
US: 20 Jay Street, Suite 1010, Brooklyn, NY 11201
versobooks.com

Verso is the imprint of New Left Books

ISBN-13: 978-1-83976-090-7
ISBN-13: 978-1-83976-101-0 (US EBK)
ISBN-13: 978-1-83976-100-3 (UK EBK)

British Library Cataloguing in Publication Data
A catalogue record for this book is available from the British Library

Library of Congress Cataloging-in-Publication Data
A catalog record for this book is available from the Library of Congress

Typeset in Fournier by MJ & N Gavan, Truro, Cornwall
Printed in the UK by CPI Group (UK) Ltd, Croydon, CR0 4YY

Contents

Introduction

In the spring of 2016, Britain was a nation still broadly convinced of its own normality. It provided a standard for how constitutional democracy should work. It possessed a media that, while far from perfect, seemed committed to giving a factual account of the key events in public life. Political power was ostensibly held to account by the scrutiny of opposition and a sceptical media. Despite the tremors of the 2008 financial crisis and the pain of austerity that followed, it appeared that economic policymaking still operated within the bounds of a technocratic consensus. When it came to political procedures, the conduct of the media and the governance of the economy, the liberal centre was still – just – in command.

The subsequent four years destroyed this self-image, rendering the ideology of liberal norm-keeping incredible. Over a period that witnessed one historic referendum, two general elections, three prime ministers, and one chaotically handled pandemic, one liberal convention after another was openly tossed aside. Gradually at first, then at an accelerating pace, basic assumptions and constraints that had governed public life and policy were discarded. The pursuit of Brexit destroyed the liberal assumption that the job of governments is to maximise economic welfare, and threw the primacy of international markets into question. Boris Johnson's decision to prorogue Parliament in September 2019 was declared unlawful by the Supreme Court, which provoked the Conservative Party to include a cryptic pledge in its subsequent manifesto to review 'the relationship between the government, parliament and the courts'.

The *Daily Mail* declared high court judges to be 'enemies of the people', after they ruled that Parliament would need to consent to the triggering of Article 50, which initiated the Brexit process. After their disappointment with Theresa May, pro-Brexit newspapers repurposed themselves as propaganda sheets for the Johnson administration, relishing the fact that the government was now led by one of their own celebrity columnists. Favours were returned, and media outlets were soon designated either friends or enemies of the government. While one set of journalists was being granted spurious 'exclusives' with a character they dutifully referred to as 'Boris', another set – Channel 4 News, the *Daily Mirror*, the *Huffington Post*, Radio 4's *Today* programme – was being denied access to government ministers and press briefings. Downing Street began issuing political threats to public service broadcasters whenever they appeared to be enjoying too much critical autonomy. One senior government source promised that they would 'whack' the BBC and radically reduce its power.

A new set of political arts was introduced into democracy along the way. In addition to the widely discussed threat of targeted online advertising and misinformation – which is alleged to have played such an important role in the 2016 referendum – political strategists grew increasingly accomplished at using comedy, confusion and distraction to undermine reasoned debate. The 2019 general election saw the Conservative Party go all out on troll tactics, such as rebranding their Twitter feed 'factcheckUK' and disseminating false rumours about Labour activists to broadcasters. The kind of political lying and propaganda that was considered shocking in June 2016 has since become viewed with weary familiarity, raising the prospect that the damage to fact-based political argument is now terminal.

Frightening evidence emerged about the attitudes and values of the newly triumphant political demographics. Brexit voters, the vast majority of whom were born before 1965, were likely to hold the kind of 'authoritarian values' associated with support for capital punishment, traditional gender hierarchies and tougher treatment of children.[1] Conservative Party members, who had the task of electing a new prime minister in summer 2019, were found to be 71 per cent male, 38 per cent over the age of sixty-six, and so obsessed with Brexit that they considered it worth sacrificing economic prosperity, the Union and even the Conservative Party for.[2] Among this primarily white, male, ageing section of English society, Islamophobia is simple common sense.

At the same time, this period witnessed the unprecedented exposure and recognition of political injustices, further contributing to the demolition of the liberal centre. The shock of Jeremy Corbyn's electoral surge in the summer of 2017, which deprived May of her parliamentary majority and set the stage for the political gridlock of the following two years, represented an overdue public affirmation that austerity was socially and politically unsustainable. It was followed immediately afterwards by the horror of the Grenfell Tower fire, which offered the most harrowing demonstration of just how unequal individual lives had become. The Windrush scandal of 2018, which saw black British citizens being terrorised by government bureaucracy and threatened with deportation (an effect of the 'Hostile Environment' immigration policy introduced in 2014), revealed a disregard for judicial norms that few had imagined the British state was capable of, at least within its own borders.

Within two months of Britain's departure from the European Union, the political establishment had been engulfed in the unprecedented chaos and horrors of the coronavirus pandemic. Johnson was forced to rein in his jocular nationalism, in an effort to look statesmanlike, serious and deferential to experts. But even then, the government couldn't resist resorting to deceptive communications tactics, as the prime minister struggled to adopt the necessary gravitas. While the crisis emerged with little warning, ultimately to do far more economic damage to Britain than Brexit, it arrived at a time when trust in the media and politicians was already at a dangerously low ebb. The National Health Service was one of the last remaining unconditional commitments that the state made to society, on which all political parties agreed. While the symbolic reverence for the NHS was ratcheted up further thanks to coronavirus, the assumption that the state could and would protect lives – so fundamental to liberal philosophy – was unable to hold.

The health crisis also did unprecedented damage to the economic institution that is more important to liberalism than any other: the labour market. For centuries, labour markets have been integral to how liberal economies meet human needs and establish social peace. For decades, welfare reforms have sought to use work (and active job-seeking) as a way of inculcating independence and greater activity. The upheavals of 2020 rendered that project utterly impossible, offering the most public and undeniable demonstration that poverty and dependence are not simply a 'choice'. This triggered the surreal spectacle of conservative politicians and newspapers debating the merits of unconditional cash transfers. In the context of rentier capitalism and what Jodi Dean terms 'neo-feudalism', the credibility of the labour market was already in decline, as the middle classes turned increasingly to assets in search of security and income.[3] The coronavirus ensured that, however the crisis of liberalism was to be resolved, it would not be built upon the familiar bedrock of the wage relation.

This litany of crises and scandals spoke of a nation and a state that no longer trusted in the liberal ideals of procedural fairness and independent judgement, and was scarcely pretending to. And yet, the status quo was not abandoned all at once; there is no single date or event that can be pinpointed as a turning point. Rather, what we can witness over the course of 2016–20 (in particular, the forty-three months that elapsed between Britain's vote to Leave and its leaving) is a series of increasingly desperate measures to harness and contain the forces of reactionary nationalism within mainstream political institutions.

In this book, I break this series down into three phases. Phase one, which lasted from the referendum through to the 2017 general election, set the template for what would follow: witnessing the populist groundswell of Brexit, Theresa May sought to hitch her leadership and party platform to it. Unable to represent (or perhaps even recognise) the full extent of the anti-political, anti-liberal anger that had fuelled Brexit in the first place, May failed to convert this into electoral success, despite her rhetorical attacks on the 'citizens of nowhere'.

Phase two lasted until March 2019, when May was forced to request an extension of Britain's membership of the European Union beyond the original two years stipulated in Article 50. In Westminster, this phase was characterised by a quagmire of government defeats in Parliament, and a steady trickle of ministerial resignations, producing an increasingly disruptive and vocal right-wing. What this phase eventually confirmed was that the centre could not hold: however the political crisis was going to be resolved, it would not be via normal representative democracy or normal political leadership. Something unusual and dangerous would be required instead, which is what the third phase witnessed. From the new Brexit Party's stunning victory in the April 2019 European elections, through the proroguing of Parliament, the December general election and Britain's successful departure from the EU in January 2020, it was clear that an abnormal type of politics had arrived.

The turmoil of phase three was eventually calmed by Johnson's electoral victory, achieved on the back of the mesmerising anti-political mantra 'Get Brexit Done' and an absence of many clear intentions beyond this. It is scarcely surprising that the populist, court-baiting, demagogic madness of those months has not been sustained as a paradigm for government. But that does nothing to suggest that the crisis is over, or that liberal normality has been restored. What was revealed in the months and years leading up to Johnson's electoral victory was that the 'liberal elites', against whom Brexit and nationalist movements are pitted, have been toppled. Or rather, more accurately, that in order for those elites to retain their power, they must be willing to sacrifice any residual commitment to liberalism, and to do so publicly.

Thus, in September 2019, the Johnson administration made the spectacular gesture of purging twenty-one anti-Brexit Conservative MPs from the party, including the 'father' of the House of Commons, Kenneth Clarke, and Sir Nicholas Soames, Winston Churchill's grandson. Others resigned from the cabinet out of concern at the direction the government was taking, including Johnson's own brother, Jo. What was revealed during these periods is something that remains true even when the turbulence has subsided; namely that, as occurred with the GOP and Donald Trump, most of the conservative establishment is willing to dump its principles for political advantage.

Meanwhile ostensibly centrist cabinet ministers, such as Matt Hancock and Nicky Morgan, turned out to be entirely comfortable with a reckless, even lawless, administration.

The sometime establishment 'paper of record', *The Times*, backed Johnson in the 2019 general election, on the basis that he should be free to act however he pleased and without warning. Its leader enthused that 'A Tory majority would free Mr Johnson to act boldly in other areas. For electoral reasons the manifesto steered clear of setting out policies on many issues that will need to be addressed in the next parliament.'[4]

The escalation of the crisis, from the referendum of 2016 through to the prorogation and propaganda of 2019, served as a useful X-ray of the once-liberal establishment. It revealed what figures such as Hancock and Morgan, and papers such as *The Times*, were prepared to stand for. The answer being: pretty much anything.

To the extent that it survives, liberalism exists now as an ethical persuasion or a cultural identity. To be sure, this makes it something that can be rallied around and identified with, as was seen with the impressive anti-Brexit marches, but liberalism loses its defining claim to universal legitimacy and consensus-formation in the process. Once institutions and norms are of only pragmatic, cosmetic, affective or instrumental value, they cease to function as institutions and norms, and become resources to be exploited. This being the case, we need to consider whether 2016 was indeed generative of such a crisis, or whether in fact it was a symptom – and a delayed one at that – of a much older crisis. How might we place 2016–20 in a longer and larger historical context? What were the underlying preconditions of this liberal collapse? How was the ground laid?

Accumulation by Distrust

The two inventions that have caused the greatest disruption within liberal democracies over the past half century are the credit derivative and the digital platform. Credit derivatives are financial instruments, first developed in the 1970s, which allow a stream of future debt repayments to be converted into an asset (that is, securitised), which can then be sold to a third party. This is supported by increasingly sophisticated credit ratings, based on surveillance and quantitative analysis of a potential borrower's behaviour. Securitisation turns the relationship between a creditor and a debtor into a commodity that can be owned by someone else altogether, who can then bundle it up with other derivatives, sell it on again and so on.

Digital platforms, such as Facebook, Uber and YouTube, are a more recent and familiar invention. The defining feature of these platforms is that they provide a social utility, which connects users to one another, and then exploits these connections for profit in a range of ways.[5] Either they exploit their users' attention to sell advertising space (as Facebook does), or they control a whole marketplace and charge sellers for using it (as Uber does). But all platforms have two features in common. Firstly, they tend towards monopolisation, seeing as users have an interest in being where all the others are. Secondly, they have vast surveillance opportunities, which they exploit for further profit. Crucially, platforms have achieved a public status that is closer to telecom companies than to publishers, meaning that they hold minimal responsibility for how their technology is used.

The chaos unleashed by these inventions is legion, and central to the story recounted in this book. The securitisation of US mortgages, plus a lucrative underestimation of the risks attached to them, triggered the 'credit crunch' of summer 2007, leading up to the crisis of 2008, bank bailouts and nationalisations, then a decade of exceptional monetary policies, austerity and wage stagnation. In the UK, the national debt doubled as a result of the bailouts and economic shock. The political response, following the election of the Coalition Government in May 2010, was to pursue aggressive cuts to welfare, local government and higher education spending.

There is compelling evidence that the cuts hit hardest in those households and parts of the country which then became most supportive of Nigel Farage and Brexit.[6] The state rescue of banks, and the abandoning of the vulnerable, made an undeniable contribution to the sense that the 'elites' look after one another, rather than acting on behalf of the public. The sentiment that society is 'broken' and that the guilty go unpunished, which is so eagerly encouraged and exploited by nationalists, received no greater endorsement than during 2008–9. Plenty of lines can be drawn between 2008 and the political upheavals of 2016.[7] The financial crisis also played a decisive role in politicising a younger generation on the left, who made an important contribution to Jeremy Corbyn's unexpected electoral surge in 2017.[8]

The effect of tech platforms on liberal democracies has been feverishly discussed. Following Britain's 2016 referendum and Trump's election victory, liberals fixated on the malign power of Facebook, Cambridge Analytica, Russian 'troll farms' and Vladimir Putin to sway election outcomes by planting 'fake news' in front of the eyeballs of easily persuaded swing voters. The lack of any editorial bottlenecks or regulation meant that a kind of information anarchy had broken out, heralding a 'post-truth' world in which nobody could tell truth from lies any longer. The fine-grained psychographic profiling techniques facilitated by Facebook meant that democracy could now be 'hacked' by targeting critical voters with precisely the right message to influence their vote.

Others are more sceptical about this narrative, asking instead why so many voters were sufficiently angry and alienated from the liberal mainstream in the first place. But regardless of one's explanation for the vote results, one thing is clearly true: the sheer quantity of content that now circulates publicly, combined with the greater difficulty of validating it, has produced new forms of political engagement and disengagement. Political passions – fandom, anti-fandom, rage, devotion – have risen, but so has a new political sensibility that treats all political and public discourse with scepticism, abandoning any effort to distinguish fact from lies. Political campaigns and the media have been sucked into this vortex.

The long-term outcome of the coronavirus crisis remains unclear. But one of the few certainties of this political and economic emergency is that digital platforms have been strengthened by it. At the same time that small businesses were disappearing at a terrifying speed, Amazon took on tens of thousands of new workers. Social life became even more dependent on the social infrastructure of platform capitalism. The same platforms that were destabilising social and political life prior to the appearance of COVID-19 became virtually preconditions of society, placing a kind of wide-ranging constitutional power in the hands of private corporations.

These are just some of the ways in which the credit derivative and the platform have transformed our political world in the twenty-first century. But there is more to it than this: they share a common logic, which eats away at integrity of public institutions. The function of both credit derivatives and of platforms is to take existing relationships built around mutuality and trust and then exploit them for profit. A loan, originally, was something that concerned two parties: the lender and the borrower. In its purest form, it depended on moral evaluations of character and honesty (judgements which were inevitably polluted by cultural, racial and gendered prejudice). Securitisation takes the debt relation that exists between two parties and turns it into an asset that yields a return. It turns a moral norm (in this case, a duty of repayment) into a commodity.

The underlying logic of a platform is the same. Facebook, YouTube and Uber take forms of mutual dependence that already exist in society, and find a way of extracting a revenue from them. These companies didn't invent friendship, cultural creation or municipal transport, but found a way to intervene in existing networks of these things in pursuit of profit. As with mortgage securitisation, they take two-way relations and insert themselves as an unnecessary third party. Along the way, they introduce scoring and ranking systems, quantifying the quality of social activity in terms of 'likes', 'shares' and stars out of five. A relationship based around trust is disrupted, and turned into one of instrumentality, strategy and self-interest.

The effect of these technologies is to drive a wedge between the 'front stage' and the 'back stage' of social and public life. The view of the world available to the general public becomes separated from that available to elites of one kind or another, breeding a disconnect between the rules, rituals and culture of everyday life and the mentality of financiers and digital technocrats. In place of the 'social contract' that was liberalism's founding article of faith, there is surveillance. The descent of the public into cynicism, mistrust and conspiracy theory, in a political system that does not make the logic and purpose of power visible, is inevitable.

This brings us face to face with the ideology and rationality of neoliberalism. Since the 1950s, American neoliberal thinkers have sought to expand the reach of economics into areas of human life that were otherwise governed by social and political norms.[9] Gary Becker's theory of 'human capital' represented education and child-rearing in terms of their future financial returns. The public choice theory of the Virginia School aimed to represent democracy and public office in terms of the calculated self-interest of those involved.[10] The Chicago School did the same in relation to law and economics. This amounts to what I've termed the 'disenchantment of politics by economics'.[11] It also generates an attitude in which the purpose of social relations is to provide data and revenue to some third party. Threaded through the technologies of the credit derivative and the

platform is a neoliberal rationality which expands the reach
of financial calculation into areas previously governed by
social norms. The rise of so-called surveillance capital in
the twenty-first century was preordained by an economic
and political rationality that dates back to the mid-twentieth
century.[12]

This is disastrous for political liberalism. Dating back
to the mid-seventeenth century, and the work of Thomas
Hobbes in particular, liberalism's key concern has been
how to artificially manufacture trust. Hobbes saw the sovereign state as an artificial entity, whose capacity to create
and enforce laws was the precondition of all peaceful, prosperous and reasonable social life. Mercantile communities,
together with the nascent financial sector of merchant banks
and coffee houses, invented their own trust devices in the
form of book-keeping techniques, on which insurance and
bond markets were based. Liberalism was born in a state of
fundamental ambivalence regarding the ultimate grounds
of public trust: law or economics?[13] Its legitimacy rested on
establishing relatively clear boundaries between the two,
separating the terrain of finance from that of politics, with
central banks serving as the mediators between the two.

The Keynesian model of the state, which prospered for
nearly thirty years after the Second World War, was developed with the explicit aim of reining in finance and bringing
it under the authority of national sovereign law. With this
established, the liberal state had the autonomy to manufacture the conditions of social cohesion, which it did through
the provision of an expanding welfare state, free education
and progressive taxation. From the 1970s onwards, however,

the neoliberal project has been to aggressively reverse this hierarchy, so that states are brought instead under the 'disciplining' authority of financial markets. Law-makers must increasingly consider their actions, not in terms of their commitment to voters or social cohesion, but in terms of how they will be judged by bond traders and currency speculators.[14] The crisis that began in 2008 represented not the end of this principle, but its most shocking affirmation.

Neoliberal reforms involved privatising, marketising and outsourcing services that had originally been created and provided by the Keynesian state on a civic basis, rather than as a matter of economic efficiency. David Harvey has referred to this as 'accumulation by dispossession', seeing as it exploits an inheritance of public and civic goods.[15] However, we might also view it as a type of 'accumulation by distrust', in that new opportunities for profit are created by casting doubt on the vocation and judgement of public service professionals. Lucrative opportunities open up for auditors and consultants, to evaluate, rate and rank schools, hospitals, councils, and even nations, according to how well they deliver 'value for money'.

Distrust and audit culture work in a vicious circle, generating a spiral of surveillance and paranoia. Once suspicions are cast on others – be they public officials, teachers or other members of our community – no amount of data will be sufficient to alleviate them. The platform economy drives this into everyday life. Reputation and recommendations systems were originally unveiled with the promise of establishing trust between strangers, for instance on eBay. But Airbnb is now increasingly plagued by the phenomenon of sellers installing secret cameras around their homes, to seek additional proof of a buyer's honesty.

The authority of language is downgraded in the process. Throughout its history, liberalism has relied on public institutions and procedures to bolster the credibility of public speech. The ideal of 'the public record', a central pillar of how facts are established and shared, assumes that public figures will be held to account and constrained by their own words. Modern science has developed exact procedures through which to measure, record and share evidence. But as neoliberalism has unleashed wave upon wave of rating, ranking, evaluation and audit processes (often conducted without transparency), publicly established facts are no longer in a position of authority. Science itself becomes judged according to calculations of financial return. It was precisely the threat that *money* posed to truth (and not some philosophical deconstruction) that prompted the diagnosis of 'postmodernism' in the 1970s.[16]

Much of what is labelled 'populism' is really a longing for some version of the state that predated neoliberal reforms. The Brexit mantra of 'take back control' may have been a dog-whistle about border control and immigration, but the appeal to national sovereignty, which clearly strikes such a chord with the baby-boomer generation, works partly because this age group can remember a time when the state was in command of its own economy and able to deliver social security to its own citizens. This gets refracted via the ugly nostalgia for cultural and ethnic homogeneity, and is exploited for political gain by politicians willing to toy with this nostalgia.

Liberal democracies have continued to hold elections, fought mostly by political parties that long predate neo-liberalism. But they have witnessed declining levels of participation, particularly from around 1990 onwards, and especially among the working class and the young.[17] In Britain, voter turn-out was over 77 per cent in the 1992 general election, but was under 60 per cent in 2005 (and under 40 per cent among under-twenty-fives). The rising autonomy – nay, sovereignty – of finance since the 1970s has been accompanied by a not unreasonable feeling that democratic institutions aren't *really* where power lies, and that politicians must therefore be in it for money or fame. A vicious circle ensues, in which voters become ever more cynical about politics and public service, and therefore ever more reliant on markets, debt and audit to undergird social life.

Neoliberalism is a system that progressively devours the conditions of social trust and converts it into revenue streams. The common attribute of credit derivatives, digital platforms and contemporary democracy is that, behind the publicly visible institutional face and the various promises and commitments on offer, there lies a hidden logic of calculation, which is ultimately in command. Institutions become a kind of cosmetic veneer, mere ritual, behind which sit financial and algorithmic machinations. Political cynicism is the logical outcome of a system that views public life as a resource to be extracted from, rather than as the stage on which justice and truth will be established. The sense that public life is now a sham, and the yearning for this to be called out (if necessary by a maniac), lie at the heart of the political movements that shook the world in 2016.

After Liberalism

The events of 2016–20, recounted in this book, are evidence of what happens as neoliberal rationality penetrates the most cherished institutions of liberalism, in particular, parliamentary democracy, party politics and the public sphere of newspapers and broadcasters. The effects are unpredictable and unstable, indeed not always recognisable as 'neoliberal' at all. Alienation from representative democracy, and distrust in the media, had been brewing for many years, as multiple surveys have confirmed. Nationalists certainly exploit these feelings of powerlessness and resentment. But as the institutions and credibility of liberalism crumble, something new fills the void. Evidence and examples of this 'something' are scattered throughout the essays contained here.

Under the neoliberal conditions I've described, all action becomes dictated by a single question; the same question, incidentally, that Donald Trump fixates on: what will this do for my ratings? How many clicks, views and likes will it provoke? How much attention will it command? How much approval will it win? As Michel Feher has persuasively argued, neoliberals might have promised a society built around entrepreneurship and self-invention, but in practice they authorised a society of perpetual audit and rating.[18] Whether it be the social media platform or the credit scoring technology (and the two are now converging), individuals constantly feel the force of rating in their everyday lives. Everything becomes about PR, a kind of perpetual performance of the kind of personality that is like-able and creditable.

We can now see the consequences of this all around us. Political leadership becomes a matter of celebrity and audience 'engagement'. Figures such as Johnson and Trump, who can draw attention towards them, driving up clicks and ratings, become a crucial asset to political parties. They also become a valued piece of 'content' for platforms and media agencies, producing new alliances between the media, political parties and ultimately the state. The business 'synergies' between the Trump White House and Fox News, co-producing a constant stream of political reality television, are palpable.[19] Johnson's relationship with the media, especially the newspapers that are read by the same ageing demographic that votes Conservative, has a similar dynamic. Despite their very different demeanours, Johnson and Trump both have a public status as reality television stars or stand-up comedians: they offer a genre of content that fuses entertainment with news.

Britain's media, and especially its newspapers, have played an active political role for many years in cultivating hostility towards immigrants, the European Union and the welfare state. Its biases are not news. But in the wake of Brexit, and imbued with the logic of the news 'feed' or 'stream', news outlets became permanent campaigns, working primarily towards 'up rating' one set of politicians and political content, and 'down rating' another. Strategic misrepresentation of others (both favourable and unfavourable) is how politics is conducted, not just by professional spin doctors, but by politicians, journalists and ordinary social media users. Far from seeking to report events, or hold power 'to account', news media (including celebrity interviewers and journalists) increasingly become part of a steady stream of unfolding events. The distinction between the reporter and the reported is muddied.

Herd-like behaviour and thinking is one effect of this. Just as financial markets are subject to irrational bubbles of sentiment (where it makes sense to buy something because everyone else is buying it), news and opinion become subject to virality and collective surges of sentiment that rise and fall like the prices of stocks. The critic (who plays such a pivotal role in the liberal vision of the public sphere, as seen by Kant and Habermas) risks being ignored or unfollowed, and is therefore replaced by the troll, who denounces and attacks for spectacular effect. This means the rise of a new type of celebrity evaluator – Piers Morgan, Brendan O'Neill, Simon Cowell – who commands clicks and views by issuing judgements crafted for maximum controversy. Similarly, a new type of celebrity rationalist – Richard Dawkins, Steven Pinker, Toby Young – emerges, to perform a pastiche of enlightenment for the benefit of fans and anti-fans.

The quest to be rated, liked and clicked is unrelenting, in what Gilles Deleuze perceptively identified in 1992 as the new 'societies of control'. The value of a given statement is in how appealing (or shocking or funny …) it seems *right now*, and not how successfully it serves as a description of the past or as a promise for the future. In this post-liberal scenario, the data archive and the algorithm are what knit together society's past, present and future, and not public speech or writing. This is what I mean when I refer in a number of essays to the switch from a society of 'facts' to one of 'data'. Whether Johnson speaks the 'truth' or not becomes an irrelevance, and the 'public record' becomes outmoded.

Leaders such as Johnson are not trusted by the public. They are not expected to keep their *word*. Such politicians prosper under conditions in which words are no longer expected to be kept. The experience of neoliberal reforms, and of austerity in particular, demonstrated that finance – and not democracy – now determines which promises will be kept. Johnson and Brexit appeal specifically to those who believe public institutions are riddled with self-interested elites and need to be ripped up. The autumn of 2019, when liberals enjoyed a wave of apparent victories via the Supreme Court and vigorous parliamentary autonomy, was a mirage. The popular fury at this assertion of constitutional norms and regulations ensured that Johnson's victory the following December was all the greater.

The impossible task confronting liberals over recent years, not just in Britain but around the world, has been to make the case for analogue techniques of record-keeping and norm-keeping, against the torrent of digital media and the outrageous, unruly, hilarious practices that it facilitates. Not only does the liberal come to appear humourless, puritanical and conservative in their commitment to public procedure and facts; they also appear slow. While the demagogic leader-entertainer is constantly changing the subject and shaping the mood, the liberal is still talking about something that happened yesterday or last year. The resentment aimed towards the 'mainstream media' and 'liberal elites' rests on the idea that their commitment to rules and facts is a cultural quirk (a symptom of over-education), and that society no longer relies on such things to cohere.

Once public institutions and norms lose credibility, so do the divisions that separate them. Liberalism was built on a series of separations: between public and private, between state and market, politics and media, and between the three branches of government (executive, legislative, judiciary). These separations have been declared a deceitful sham by feminist and Marxist critics among others, on the basis that they work in the interests of patriarchy and/or capital. But they are also undone by neoliberal policy reforms, which seek to bring all of social and political life under the gaze of a blanket financial audit. In the context of the 'internet of things', and the fusing of credit rating with platforms, neoliberalism could yet issue in an infrastructure not unlike that of the Chinese 'social credit' scoring system, where all behaviour – public or private, social or economic – can be captured as proof of character.

As these structural shifts are underway below the surface, so once-separate public institutions and jurisdictions begin to blur into one. Just as the separation of business and state was dissolved under the reforms of the 1980s and '90s, and as the distinction between journalism and political campaigning fades, the very idea of power being 'held to account' by an independent, separate judge or critic of some kind becomes less plausible and then suspicious. What does the judge want? What is their agenda? Whose side are they on? Deteriorating trust in public institutions breeds animosity towards outsiders and those perceived as disloyal. This is how the collapse of liberalism produces the conditions of nationalism, and even of fascism. The assertion of a single national (or ethno-national) 'people', which unites government, media, business and public around a common destiny, is the ultimate PR victory. Who gets eliminated or discarded, in order for this bubble of mutual rating and liking to be achieved, is another question.[20]

Real-time Sociology

The essays collected in this book, which are grouped together in three chapters, were all written during the interregnum between Britain's 2016 referendum and its 2020 departure from the European Union. This was a disorientating and fast-moving period in the nation's politics, when many of the most dependable building blocks of liberal democracy seemed to be disintegrating. From the first piece, a blogpost written the morning after the referendum, through to the last, a column written after Johnson's 2019 election victory, they are all efforts to make sense of what is unfolding, in something close to real-time. What they inevitably lack in quantity of hindsight, I hope they make up for in their immediacy, which grants a sense of how things appeared at the time.

There are various preoccupations throughout, that have already been highlighted: the abandoning of liberal economic rationality, the declining authority of empirical facts, the mainstreaming of nationalism, the hatred of 'liberal elites', the effect of big data and real-time media on our politics, the new mould of celebrity leaders, the crisis of democratic representation. These are all linked in ways that I've endeavoured to show. The over-arching theme is of a shift from a liberal polity based around norms, laws, expertise and institutions to a neoliberal one based around algorithmic surveillance and financial calculation.

The task for the kind of 'real-time sociology' that I was engaged in with these essays is to straddle the fast-moving world of the news cycle (which has grown significantly faster in the twenty-first century) with the search for under-lying structures and conditions.[21] This is not unlike the kind of 'conjunctural analysis' that Gramscians have long aimed at, and for which Stuart Hall's work has been the model. Hall always encouraged us to pay attention to the new and unprecedented, and not simply view history as a predict-able unfolding of underlying mechanics. Many of the essays in this volume perform a kind of brokerage service, mov-ing between unfamiliar and shocking political events and familiar social and political theories, including many of the classics – Marx, Hirschman, Arendt, Foucault, Weber. In scurrying back and forth between my Twitter feed and my bookshelves, the hope is that we *can* understand what's going on, without either wishful thinking or denial of the genuine conjunctural novelty.

There are obvious risks attached to theorising events like this. You can make a bad call, miss the wood for the trees, be duped by hype or by paranoia. I've never pretended to be much good at predictions, which I leave to the quantitative political scientists (my estimations of Theresa May's elec-toral prowess were as wrong as anyone's). But I think it's important that we at least try to relate the flux of the pres-ent to the underlying conditions, which are more durable.

When everything appears to be changing and unprecedented, it's all the more important to find the continuities and precedents, without downplaying the shock of the new. One of the most dramatic transformations to have taken hold of public life in Western democracies in the twenty-first century is the way it potentially becomes 'consumed' as a constant 'stream' of content, relying on a combination of outrage and humour to hold and sway its audience. All academic disciplines offer a pause button of sorts, because they necessarily require slow and careful consideration of a moment in time, and can't dwell in perpetual flow. But only sociology helps to explain where the acceleration arose from in the first place, on the assumption that *something* must be driving and structuring an apparently chaotic and reckless process.

1

'The People Have Spoken'

The shock of the EU referendum result prompted outrage and panic within the liberal establishment. Did truth not count any longer? Why had the tabloids been allowed to fan the anti-European flames for so long? Was the economy going to fall off a cliff? In the immediate aftermath of the referendum, there was bewilderment and fear regarding the loss of political stability and the emergence of an apparently kamikaze nationalist force. The entire era of globalisation – cultural and economic – seemed to have come to a sudden halt. Within three weeks of the referendum, Theresa May was installed as the new prime minister, and immediately set out a new type of Conservative programme, ostensibly sympathetic to the sentiments of the 'left behind'. Apparently, now in the safe hands of the former home secretary, the protective, punitive state was back. For just under a year, cheered to the rafters by the Daily Mail *and much of her own party, she sought to channel the passions of Brexit to expand her authority. So high was her confidence by the spring of 2017, that she did the very thing she had promised not to do: call an early election.*

Initial Ruptures

It became clear early on in the night of the referendum that Leave had extraordinary levels of support in the North East, taking 70 per cent of the votes in Hartlepool and 61 per cent in Sunderland. It subsequently emerged that Wales had voted for Leave overall, especially strongly in the South around areas such as Newport. It is easy to focus on the recent history of Tory-led austerity when analysing this, as if anger towards elites and immigrants was simply an effect of the public spending cuts of the previous six years or (more structurally) the collapse of Britain's pre-2007 debt-driven model of growth.

But consider the longer history of these regions as well. They are well recognised as Labour's historic heartlands, sitting on coalfields and/or around ship-building cities. Indeed, outside of London and Scotland, they were among the only blobs of Labour red on the 2015 electoral map. There is no reason to think that they should not stay red in a future election. But in the language of Marxist geographers, they have had no successful 'spatial fix' since the stagflation crisis of the 1970s. Thatcherism gutted them with pit closures and monetarism, but generated no private sector jobs to fill the space. The entrepreneurial investment that neoliberals always believe is just around the corner never materialised.

New Labour's solution was to spread wealth in their direction using fiscal policy: public sector back-office jobs were strategically relocated to South Wales and the North East to alleviate deindustrialisation, while tax credits made low-productivity service work more socially viable. This effectively created a shadow welfare state that was never publicly spoken of, co-existing with a political culture that heaped scorn on dependency. The infamous comment, sometimes attributed to Peter Mandelson, that the Labour heartlands could be depended on to vote Labour no matter what 'because they've got nowhere else to go', spoke of a dominant attitude. In Nancy Fraser's terms, New Labour offered 'redistribution' but no 'recognition'.[1]

This cultural contradiction wasn't sustainable and nor was the geographic one. Not only was the 'spatial fix' relatively short term, seeing as it depended on rising tax receipts from the South East and a centre-left government willing to spread money quite lavishly (albeit discreetly), it also failed to deliver what many of those Brexit voters perhaps crave the most: the dignity of being self-sufficient, not necessarily in a neoliberal sense, but certainly in a communal, familial and fraternal sense.

By the same token, it seems unlikely that voters in these regions (or Cornwall or other economically peripheral spaces) would feel 'grateful' to the EU for subsidies. Knowing that your business, farm, family or region is dependent on the beneficence of wealthy liberals is unlikely to be a recipe for satisfaction. More bizarrely, the regions with the closest economic ties to the EU in general (and not just of the subsidised variety) were the most likely to vote Leave. While it may be one thing for an investment banker to understand that they 'benefit from the EU' in regulatory terms, it is quite another to encourage poor and culturally marginalised people to feel grateful towards the elites that sustain them through handouts, month by month.

Resentment develops not in spite of this generosity, but arguably because of it. This isn't to discredit what the EU does in terms of redistribution, but pointing to handouts is a psychologically and politically naive basis on which to justify remaining in the EU.

In this context, the Vote Leave campaign slogan 'take back control' was a piece of political genius. It worked on every level from the macroeconomic to the psychoanalytic. Think of what it means on an individual level to rediscover *control*. To be a person without control (for instance to suffer incontinence or a facial tick) is to be the butt of cruel jokes, to be potentially embarrassed in public. It potentially reduces one's independence. What was so clever about the language of the Leave campaign was that it spoke directly to this feeling of inadequacy and embarrassment, then promised to eradicate it. The promise had nothing to do with economics or policy, but everything to do with the psychological allure of autonomy and self-respect. Nigel Farage's political strategy was to take seriously communities who'd otherwise been taken for granted for much of the past fifty years.

This doesn't necessarily have to translate into nationalistic pride or racism (although it might well do), but it does at the very least mean no longer being laughed at. Those who have ever laughed at 'chavs' (such as the millionaire stars of *Little Britain*) have something to answer for right now. The willingness of Nigel Farage to weather the scornful laughter of metropolitan liberals (for instance through his periodic appearances on *Have I Got News For You*) could equally have made him look brave in the eyes of many potential Leave voters. I can't help feeling that every smug, liberal, snobbish barb that Ian Hislop threw Farage's way on that increasingly hateful programme was ensuring that revenge would be all the greater, once it arrived. The giggling, from which Boris Johnson also benefited handsomely, needs to stop.

Brexit reflects a much deeper cultural and political malaise, one that also appears to be driving the rise of Donald Trump in the US. Among people who have utterly given up on the future, political movements don't *need* to promise any desirable and realistic change. If anything, they are more comforting and trustworthy if predicated on the notion that the future is beyond rescue, for that chimes more closely with people's private experiences. The discovery of the 'Case Deaton effect' in the US – unexpectedly high mortality rates among white working classes – is linked to rising alcohol and opiate abuse and to rising suicide rates. It has also been shown to correlate closely to geographic areas with the greatest support for Trump.[2] It seems clear that – beyond the rhetoric of 'Great Britain' and 'democracy' – Brexit was never really articulated as a viable policy, and only ever as a destructive urge, which some no doubt now feel guilty for giving way to.

Thatcher and Reagan rode to power by promising a brighter future, which never quite materialised other than for a minority with access to elite education and capital assets. The contemporary populist promise to make Britain or America 'great again' is not made in the same way. It is not a pledge or a policy platform; it's not to be measured in terms of results. When made by the likes of Boris Johnson, it's not even clear if it's meant seriously or not. It's more an offer of a collective real-time hallucination, that can be indulged in like a video game.

The Remain campaign continued to rely on forecasts, warnings and predictions, in the hope that eventually people would be dissuaded from 'risking it'. But to those who have given up on the future already, this is all just more political rhetoric. In any case, the entire practice of modelling the future in terms of 'risk' has lost credibility, as evidenced by the now terminal decline of opinion polling as a tool for political control.

The failure of 'facts'

One of the complaints made most frequently by liberal commentators, economists and media pundits was that the referendum campaign was being conducted without regard to 'truth'. This isn't quite right. It was conducted without adequate regard to *facts*. To the great frustration of the Remain campaign, their 'facts' never cut through, whereas Leave's statistics (most famously the £350 million/week price tag of EU membership) were widely accepted.

What is a 'fact' exactly? Mary Poovey argues that a new way of organising and perceiving the world came into existence at the end of the fifteenth century with the invention of double-entry book-keeping.[3] This new style of knowledge is that of *facts*, representations that seem both context-independent, but also magically slot seamlessly into multiple contexts as and when they are needed. The basis for this magic is that measures and methodologies (such as accounting techniques) become standardised, but then treated as apolitical, thereby allowing numbers to move around freely in public discourse without difficulty or challenge. In order for this to work, the infrastructure that produces 'facts' needs careful policing, ideally through centralisation in the hands of statistics agencies or elite universities (the rise of commercial polling in the 1930s was already a challenge to the authority of 'facts' in this respect).

This game has probably been up for some time. As soon as media outlets start making a big deal about the *facts* of a situation, for instance with 'fact check' bulletins, it is clear that numbers have already become politicised. 'Facts' (such as statistics) survived as an authoritative basis for public and democratic deliberation for most of the 200 years following the French Revolution. But the politicisation of social sciences, metrics and policy administration means that the 'facts' produced by official statistical agencies must now compete with other conflicting 'facts'. The deconstruction of 'facts' has been partly pushed by varieties of postmodern theory since the 1960s, but it is also an inevitable effect of the attempt (beloved of New Labour) to turn policy into a purely scientific exercise.

The attempt to reduce politics to a utilitarian science (most often, to neoclassical economics) eventually back-fires, once the science in question then starts to become politicised. 'Evidence-based policy' is now far too long in the tooth to be treated entirely credulously, and people tacitly understand that it often involves a lot of 'policy-based evidence'. When the Remain camp appealed to their 'facts', forecasts and models, they hoped that these would be judged to be outside of the fray of politics. More absurdly, they seemed to imagine that the opinions of bodies such as the IMF might be viewed as 'independent'. Economics has been such a crucial prop for political authority over the past thirty-five years that it is now anything but outside of the fray of politics.

In place of facts, we now live in a world of *data*. Instead of trusted measures and methodologies being used to produce numbers, a dizzying array of numbers is produced by default, to be mined, visualised, analysed and interpreted however we wish. If risk modelling (using notions of statistical normality) was the defining research technique of the nineteenth and twentieth centuries, sentiment analysis is the defining one of the emerging digital era. We no longer have stable, 'factual' representations of the world, but unprecedented new capacities to sense and monitor what is bubbling up where, who's feeling what, what's the general vibe.

Financial markets are themselves far more like tools of sentiment analysis (representing the *mood* of investors) than producers of 'facts'. This is why it was so absurd to look to currency markets and spread-betters for the truth of what would happen in the referendum: they could only give a sense of what certain people felt would happen in the referendum at certain times. Given the absence of any trustworthy facts (in the form of polls), they could then only provide a sense of how investors felt about Britain's national mood: a sentiment regarding a sentiment. As the 23 June 2016 turned into 24 June, it became manifestly clear that prediction markets are little more than an aggregative representation of the same feelings and moods that one might otherwise detect via Twitter. They're not in the business of truth-telling, but of mood-tracking.

What Sort of Crisis Is This?

The bankruptcy of Lehman Brothers in September 2008 was an emergency. This was manifest in its rapid pace and the threat that it might spread exponentially, just like a fire. While the warning signs had been present for over a year prior to the collapse of Lehmans, the emergency occurred over a series of hours, and demanded an immediate policy response. The state acted as a fire brigade on the basis that the emergency would otherwise have spiralled out of control. The fact that the financial crisis may have cost a sum of money comparable to a world war does not mean the rescue wasn't worth it, if the alternative was total social meltdown.

Brexit has a completely different rhythm, which is why comparisons to Lehmans don't reveal very much. The weirdest thing about the week following the referendum has been the eerie sense of waiting for something to happen, the collapse of sterling notwithstanding. All that's happened so far is pretty much exactly what experts and policymakers predicted, whereas the experts were temporarily stumped during September 2008. Investors aren't panicking right now, they're simply responding as everyone said they would. It's the long-term future that is much more worrying. If Lehmans was a housefire (which was spreading), this is more like someone choosing to buy a house that the surveyor has found to be suffering long-term subsidence, but going ahead with the purchase anyway. Not only do the emergency services not care, they can't help you anyway. Meanwhile your insurance company (who you never liked in the first place) told you repeatedly they couldn't underwrite it.

Where they are framed as such, emergencies can be used to entrench the status quo even more firmly, making a situation *more* reliant on existing powers rather than less. This is clearly what happened with neoliberalism from 2008 onwards: states and banks benefited from the ultra-fast pace of economic meltdown in being able to implement measures (often with little deliberation, sometimes overnight or over weekends) that would rescue the status quo. Hence, states successfully sustained the flawed model of capitalism which privileged the financial sector for another eight years, while pushing the costs elsewhere. But Brexit is a crisis of the state first and foremost. This makes it slower but ultimately far more transformative and frightening.

The question is, what is the relation between the economic crisis of 2008 and the political one of 2016, and why the delay between the two? The first thing to note is that the 'emergency' of 2008 was never allowed to become a proper *crisis*, in the sense of a turning point or conclusive judgement. It was bad and scary, but in rescuing the situation, policymakers ensured that nothing would fundamentally change. Crucially, the nature of the rescue (and subsequent policies such as negative interest rates, austerity measures, national bailout and quantitative easing) meant that debt obligations were upheld at all costs. Rather than learn from the mistakes of the past and start afresh (through debt write-offs and bankruptcies) in a different direction, this absolutist respect for debts means that the power relations of the past (between creditor and debtor) are sustained and exacerbated. To insist on the sanctity of debt obligations is a way of ensuring that politics and economics are safely insulated from one another, thereby ensuring that an economic disaster avoids becoming a fully fledged crisis. This insulation was time-limited: in the UK, it turns out to have lasted eight years.

Given that the post-2008 regime of regulation, corporate governance and growth was roughly the same as the pre-2008 one, it should always have been clear that 2008 would be the first 'prong' of a two-pronged crisis. Most critical observers suspected that the second 'prong' would be similar to the first: another collapse in the credibility of financial derivatives, only this time without the same possibilities for a sovereign rescue. That would necessarily have produced far-reaching political change, for the simple reason that another rescue of the status quo wouldn't have been viable.

Instead, crisis has emanated from outside of the financial sector altogether, from democracy itself. For Britain, June 2016 might provide the full-stop at the end of a paragraph that began with September 2008 (or arguably a year earlier with Northern Rock). Historians may well look at Lehmans and Brexit as entangled with each other in various ways, but the exact causal connections between the first and second 'prongs' of the capitalist crisis are far from clear. What I think we can say instead is that both are consequences of the rise of finance from the 1980s onwards.

The term 'financialisation' refers to various processes whereby the logic of finance permeates the non-financial economy and society. All manner of economic and non-economic entities (such as higher education and homes) become valued in terms of their capacity to earn future returns on investment. Giovanni Arrighi argued that all phases of national capitalist expansion eventually reach their peak, then experience a compensatory wave of financial expansion as they go into decline.[4] This grants a national economic power a few more years of wealth accumulation, but on the basis of shifting paper around and mediating financial agreements, rather than producing things of any use. This is a case of buying time.[5]

The rampant expansion of Britain's financial sector from the 1980s onwards did exactly this, drawing money towards London (and to some extent the UK), but only on the basis that this is where money is made and traded, rather than because of productive activity. Hence, combating inflation and protecting sterling (that is, demonstrating respect for money as a good in itself) were the pivotal instruments of British industrial policy from Thatcher through to Cameron. That ended last Thursday.

Buying a few more years of prosperity via the financial sector carries severe social costs. In particular, it produces some very awkward cultural and political divisions. These never quite resemble traditional class divisions, as between 'bourgeoisie' and 'proletariat' (where the former exploits the labour power of the latter). Instead, those who happen to own assets (often thanks to family inheritance) do vastly better than those that don't. Where they choose to leverage these assets to buy more assets, then their advantages can grow exponentially. What begins with a slice of luck can

rapidly snowball into a new rentier class (the '1 per cent').[6]
The liberal attempt to anchor economic inequalities in differences in 'merit' or 'talent' or 'effort' comes under greater
and greater strain, until eventually it loses credibility altogether. The market loses its status as a 'level playing field',
producing an ideological crisis.

Furthermore, it produces a sense of intergenerational
conflict that is equally difficult to crowbar into traditional
class divisions. Certain individuals now seem hugely privileged, simply by virtue of being born between 1940 and
1970, while subsequent generations seem to do progressively worse. The current focus on 'generations' imposes
sharp dividing lines of the sort that market researchers tend
to like (such as 'baby-boomers' against 'millennials'), but
exaggerates the binary nature of the politics. Underneath
this is steady asset price inflation, *year on year*, and declining
social provision, both enabled by the steady expansion of
credit in circulation. In the UK, it becomes less economically fortunate to be born with each year that passes.

While the underlying inequalities wrought by finance
may not fall neatly into binary oppositions, they seem to
have influenced the politics of Remain versus Leave in certain ways. Leave voters consisted roughly of those who
have already accumulated assets over their lives plus some
who are unlikely to ever do so. Remain voters consisted of
those who still feel (for whatever reason) that they *could*
make financialisation work for them, either because they're
young or because they're still benefiting from asset appre-
ciation. To put that another way, many of the first group
would view money as debt (closing down the future) while

many of the latter would view it as credit (opening it up). Throw educational inequalities into this financial mix, and you get some stark political and cultural divisions.

The culture wars have entered British politics in dramatic fashion. As in the US, the divide can also be approximately traced in terms of those *with* a university degree versus those *without* one. Statistically speaking, having a university degree makes one more likely to be supportive of immigration and membership of the European Union. Those with a degree live lives that are further-reaching in geography and opportunity, lives that are broader in cultural and economic scope. The situation in America is clearly highly charged right now, but it can at least be seen in terms of a trajectory that started with Nixon, gained momentum with *Roe v Wade* and was then seized as a conscious political strategy by the Republican Party the whole way through to the madness of Donald Trump.

The shock of Brexit is partly in the discovery that this has crept up on us. Unlike America, Britain has always known that it is a class society. It speaks openly of class, makes jokes about class, judges people in terms of class. But our assumptions about class are sorely anachronistic, and don't reflect the post-'68 culture wars. We still have a major political party called the *Labour* Party. We can cope with the idea of some people being aristocrats and others being proles; at least we have a language to represent it. But the real inequalities and conflicts of post-1970s Britain, determined by a combination of finance and educational differences, have been papered over by national tradition and media ignorance. They were concealed brilliantly by the Blairite triangulation, and simply bubbled away in the background as a result.

In the US, the culture wars became reflected in the party system. Broadly speaking, the Republican Party came to represent those who felt threatened by the new freedoms of the 1960s, while the Democratic Party stood for those who felt emancipated by them. Naturally, there are some curious coalitions (the Democrats combining Wall Street with most ethnic minorities, and so on) but they have some underlying coherence. This produces a horribly aggressive politics, but it at least means representative democracy sits on top of some real sociological divides.

In the UK, the referendum on Europe was arguably the first time since the 1970s that this primal sociological divide attained any explicit democratic visibility. It took us by surprise, and showed quite how unrepresentative the delineation of 'Labour' and 'Conservative' had become, in comparison to the cultural and socio-economic divides revealed by the referendum. New Labour's insistence that *half* of the population (why *half*, exactly?) should go to university could have been a warning bell. The division between Leave and Remain has a kind of sociological weightiness that renders the familiar, comforting visions of Labour versus Tory a little superficial by comparison. Moreover, that Leave/Remain divide cuts the parties straight down the middle, rendering them both seemingly unsustainable right now.

As the chaotic dual-party leadership battles are demonstrating, Brexit already appears to be shrinking the quantity of centralised political power in the UK. For libertarians or revolutionary Marxists (enthusiastic Leave voters) this is a welcome outcome, and these intellectuals might be able to mount a coherent case for Brexit on that basis. If that were the only source of historic transformation, then it might be as much exciting as worrying. But what happens when an emergency hits in this context of crisis? This is what the intellectuals (such as Dominic Cummings) on the Leave side are completely ignoring. The justification for Brexit might just withstand the various costs that were predictable, such as a run on sterling and the loss of regional or science funding. But when an unpredictable shock occurs, we will discover what kind of political economy we are now living with and seeking security from.

The source of the emergency could be anything, but it is surely likely to be either another financial shock or a major security event. Were either of these two things to happen, the loss of political power delivered by Brexit would produce far higher levels of panic, and far greater flight towards informal and cultural sources of security: fascism and local violence. We've already witnessed the rise of public racism and harassment on Britain's streets since 23 June, and that's *without* anything yet fundamentally changing. As it becomes clear that the state's capacity to provide security (social, economic, physical) is shrinking, especially in areas where fiscal policy and EU funds were key to social cohesion, then things are likely to get worse.

Avoiding such an emergency may be crucial to how Brexit turns out. The longer we go without one, the easier it will be to absorb if and when it arrives. Anything the state could do in the meantime to guarantee equal security for all UK residents and to rule out deportations would be welcome, which makes the silence of the Home Secretary Theresa May all the more appalling. Some sort of 'Lexit' strategy might even become plausible if a period of relative peace is long enough, though it seems even less thought-through than Brexit itself. An emergency is bound to come at some point, indeed the worry must be that Brexit heightens the chance of it occurring, as existing techniques of government and prevention are buffeted by uncertainties and further austerity. Talk of fascism, violence and panic may feel over-wrought right now. But to assume these things *begin* in the same dramatic fashion with which they end is to fall into the trap of understanding history only in retrospect.

The Eurosceptic Imaginary

Given that Brexit was an event imagined and delivered from within the Conservative Party, it is worth reflecting on the longer history of Conservative Euroscepticism, dating back to the early 1990s. Firstly, the political plausibility of Brexit increased as a direct response to Tony Blair's dogmatic assumption that European integration was a historical destiny, which encompassed the UK. No doubt a figure such as Blair would have discovered a messianic agenda under any historical circumstances. But given that he gained power specifically in the mid-'90s, he was one palpable victim of the *fin de siècle* ideology (stereotyped by Francis Fukuyama's 'end of history' thesis, but also present in Anthony Giddens's 'Third Way') that the world was programmed to converge around a single political system.

Neoconservative faith in violent 'democratisation' was Blair's worst indulgence on this front, but a view of European unification (and expansion) as *inevitable* was partially responsible for inciting the Tory reaction within Westminster. Europe could have been viewed as a particular historical path, adopted in view of the particular awfulness of the European twentieth century. Instead, in a Hegelian fashion, the idea of Europe became entangled with the idea of 'globalisation', and the conservative reaction was to refuse both.

Secondly, Tory Brexiteers view the EU as an anti-market project which blocks economic freedom. This is weirdly ahistorical. Firstly, the EU was established specifically to entrench the market as the organising principle of European coordination, as a way of preventing further war between France and Germany. When the left complains that the EU is a 'neoliberal' institution that elevates the market above national democracy, this is correct. The left should recognise that, in terms of its foundational goal, it's been remarkably successful.

Of course, it achieves the single market through a high level of bureaucratic and technocratic planning (such as anti-trust, standardisation, consumer protection), allowing it to be represented as 'socialist' by those who cling to a Victorian or anarchic idea of what the market should look like. But there is no contradiction between technocracy and market competition, indeed the latter has depended on the former ever since the rise of business corporations and market regulation in the final decades of the nineteenth century.

One of the many illusions on which Brexit is based, therefore, is that capitalism is a system that works in the spaces *outside of* regulation, and that regulation is consequently anti-capitalist. A more realistic view is that *capitalism is regulation* (of working life, product standardisation, consumer choice, of markets, credit and so on), regulation that has always depended on the state – tacitly in the pre-1870 era, but explicitly ever since. The idea that, say, pharmaceuticals, financial services or business services (all areas of some lingering success for the UK) thrive in the absence of rules is to ignore the myriad ways in which it is only rules which make such industries possible in the first place. Moreover, the idea that markets can straddle multiple national jurisdictions without additional technocratic management is yet more magical thinking.

Paraphrasing Stalin, the utopia of Brexit might best be summed up as that of 'Liberalism in One Country'. The ideal is a laissez-faire of the mid-nineteenth century variety, which either destroys or disregards the ways in which this is no longer realistic. It also involves disregarding the sense in which Victorian laissez-faire was never Liberalism in One Country in the first place, but depended on empire and slavery. Brexit is therefore fuelled by a combination of destructive and fantastical urges: aspects of capitalism which resist the ideal of Victorian laissez-faire must either be got rid of (such as EU membership itself) or simply ignored. The critical question is which aspects of contemporary British capitalism fall into the former camp, and which will fall into the latter.

Overshooting the mark

Brexit represents a reaction against various models and aspects of liberalism. 'Lexit' is promoted as a route out of *neo*liberalism. Conservative campaigners for Leave were reacting partly against the calculated advice and predictions of elite economists and business leaders that Brexit would lead to recession and long-term decline. Most significantly, perhaps, Brexit was represented as a rejection of international multiculturalism and a reassertion of national difference.

All of these are refusals of dominant orthodoxies, with various histories. Lexiteers want to overturn the dominant policy orthodoxy of the past forty years, presumably so as to return to a more democratic capitalism or socialism. Leave campaigners were rejecting the dominant elite faith in economics, statistics and 'facts' that was a rising feature of politics over the twentieth century. And UKIP were demanding a radical re-localisation of law, human rights and labour markets, so as to privilege indigenous entitlements.

The fear is that, in targeting these various aspects of liberalism, some of which are relatively recent, Brexiteers have hugely overshot the mark; they have also turned the tide on one of the most basic principles of political economy: that prosperity is achieved through greater social and spatial interconnectedness. In seeking to overthrow the policies and developments of recent decades, they've shot a hole in a programme that dates the whole way back to Adam Smith in the eighteenth century. Despite the fact that few of our politicians (and even fewer of our civil servants) want this, Britain is about to adopt a strategy of national mercantilism that Smith was seeking to dissuade rulers from in 1776.

To put this another way, Brexit will result in a form of protectionism for the UK, whether it wants it or not. Protectionism can, of course, yield economic benefits and has been adopted by most rising industrial powers at key strategic junctures. It exists today, for example, in the way the United States pushes aggressive intellectual property rights in order to protect Hollywood. It helps rapidly developing and industrialising nations catch up with others. But in order to make any sense at all, there has to be something worth protecting. What does Britain have? Michael Porter's 1990 *Competitive Advantage of Nations* includes a bleak table on areas of world-leading national strategic advantage. USA: software, entertainment industries, micro-processors. Germany: machine tools, cars. Britain? *Finance and biscuits*. Like a dog refusing to give up its stick, we've staked our national pride on clinging onto things that nobody else much wants.

Two possible futures present themselves, one of which is socially regressive, the other of which is fantastical. The socially regressive one is that Britain regains a form of competitiveness by slashing taxes on mobile capital and social protections, such as the minimum wage, as has already been mooted by various Tories. This still seems likely to me, which makes Theresa May's surprisingly social democratic leadership platform another likely example of post-truth politics in action (there is no manifesto or other mechanism to hold her to any of her ideas, and it is difficult to see them surviving a recession). This achieves Liberalism in One Country by diving headlong into the past.

The second is the Steve Hilton and Dominic Cummings fantasy in which Britain hurls itself into some technologically

expansive, anarchic, cyber-utopian future. Britain becomes
a kind of experiment in new fusions of technology, science,
policy and regulation, driven by entrepreneurs whose main
ambition is to destroy the status quo. It revels in a post-truth
landscape, busting the cartel of established scientific and
business centres. According to this ideology, the only way
to discover the new is to forcefully abandon the old, no matter how many accepted truths or values are lost along the
way. Smashing up the nation state is the first step towards
smashing up vested interests in business, universities and
cultural production. This is the vision of the 'outer right' –
libertarian ideologists weaned on third-hand versions of
Nietzsche and Schumpeter – who are quite content to view
a nation as a laboratory to mess around in.

The key question is what happens when these various
ideals collide with the reality of British capitalist society in
the twenty-first century. The immediate fall-out has been
ugly: a 500 per cent rise in reported racial hate crime, British
researchers being dumped from European research projects,
and early signs of economic decline. But how might 'Liberalism in One Nation' work in real sociological terms?
I think we can envisage it playing out differently in three
strata of economic activity and social class.

Firstly, there are the businesses which lined up against
Brexit, because they trade with Europe, value steady and
generally reasonable market rules, and don't want politics
to interfere with their investment strategies. The national
'home' of these businesses is often irrelevant, other than
for tax purposes, and their place in Britain is often via foreign direct investment. It is difficult to imagine any aspect

of Brexit that benefits these businesses. From the perspective of a multinational corporation, far from overthrowing the 'burden of red tape' (as Brexiteers believe), Britain is now in the process of building a new wall of inefficiency around itself.

In economic jargon, the 'transaction costs' of locating in and doing business with Britain will rise permanently as a result of Brexit. Regulatory inefficiencies benefit one class of business only: the intermediaries and consultants who sell services in managing these transaction costs (a 'Brexit management industry' is surely going to arise, just like a minister for Brexit).[7] International capital will be greatly inconvenienced by Brexit, but that simply means that less of it will travel to or via Britain in the future. Global capitalism is fast and complex. By comparison, Britain has chosen to become slow and complicated. The Conservative right is about to discover that, for multinational corporations located in Britain, there is one thing worse than being regulated by Brussels, and that is not being regulated by Brussels.

Secondly, there are those uber-elite individuals who still dwell in Blair's *fin de siècle* bubble of a single open global society, including Blair himself. Blair has said that he cannot understand the rise of Bernie Sanders and Jeremy Corbyn.[8] Presumably he is even more flummoxed by the Brexit vote, and especially by how it sucked in quasi-Blairites such as Michael Gove. Blair's myopia has many possible explanations. But one is that people like him do genuinely now inhabit a borderless global space, in which laws, regulations and policies are only ever things to be viewed from above, and never things one is forced into accepting.

Brexit may make London a less attractive destination for the global super-rich (the 0.001 per cent or so), a class that includes Blair. This would be no bad thing. However, it should also be recognised that this class is defined partly by its ability to buy its way out of jurisdictional limits when it needs to. 'Citizenship services' mean that passports can be bought; 'tax efficiency services' mean that the mega-wealthy can avoid ever having to pay for local social goods; 'family offices' exist to manage the international affairs (houses, education, leisure) of super-rich families. So long as these services exist, decisions about national sovereignty and international law have relatively little effect on the freedom of the extremely rich. The extremely wealthy are Brexit-proof.

The worry must be that, in a stagnant economy, politicians will be tempted to formally recognise the privileges that this class possesses. This means accepting that they won't pay their tax in full, granting them the residency rights that they desire, relieving them of inconvenient obligations to be transparent (of the sort the EU might have imposed, in relation to money-laundering, say). All of this would be in the hope that these people continue to spend time in post-Brexit Britain and splash some of their cash around.

Finally there is the class that has become known as the 'precariat', which will surely expand in post-Brexit Britain. The vote against immigration was really a vote against a multicultural precariat: the eastern and southern Europeans who do relatively low-wage, low-security work in the UK. We still don't know the future of these migrants or how far their numbers will reduce in future. Given that immigration tends to rise and fall in correlation to economic growth, perhaps Brexit will achieve reduced immigration after all. But if there is further austerity, as George Osborne declared inevitable in the event of Brexit, that will mean more people are forced into contingent forms of wage labour. This is where various elements of the right currently converge, around the idea of increased employment through reduced workplace rights. There are various aggressive neoliberal aspects of the current Tory policy agenda that haven't gone anywhere.

There is one emerging economic model that ties all of these strands together, satisfying regressive nineteenth-century liberals, techno-utopian libertarians, communitarian conservatives, corporate elites and policy pragmatists equally. This is the cluster of platforms and services known as the 'sharing economy'. These seek to push a *rentier* mentality into more and more corners of society, making the ownership of assets (homes, bedrooms, cars, capital equipment, free time, and so on) the condition of an income.

The opportunities for the precariat to be administered and employed via digital platforms have only just begun to be explored, but have huge potential. This fulfils a liberal dream of allowing labour to find its 'correct' price in an entirely flexible, maximally liquid market, just as financial markets do for shares and bonds according to the Efficient Markets Hypothesis. I would expect this argument to gain new momentum over the coming years, advanced as much by those with a regressive fantasy of liberal Victoriana as by those with a techno-utopian fantasy of capitalist upheaval.

Outside of Nigel Farage's local pub, where people dream that their warm beer breaks EU rules and take pride in refusing to wear seatbelts on their drive home, modern societies are never unregulated. The irony of liberalism after Brexit is that, in sticking up two fingers to the regulatory power of the unelected technocrats in Brussels, it probably hastens the regulatory advance of invisible and unspoken algorithms in Silicon Valley corporations. For Steve Hilton, happily resident in prosperous multicultural northern California, surrounded by a coterie of venture capitalists and the anti-democratic digerati, his long-distance support for Brexit makes perfect sense.

The Crisis of Statistical Fact

In theory, statistics should help settle arguments. They ought to provide stable reference points that everyone – no matter what their politics – can agree on. Yet in recent years, divergent levels of trust in statistics have opened up one of the key schisms in Western liberal democracies. Shortly before the 2016 presidential election, a study in the US discovered that 68 per cent of Trump supporters distrusted the economic data published by the Federal Government. In the UK, a research project by Cambridge University and YouGov looking at conspiracy theories discovered that 55 per cent of the population believes that the government 'is hiding the truth about the number of immigrants living here'.[9]

Rather than diffusing controversy and polarisation, it seems as if statistics are actually stoking them. Antipathy

to statistics has become one of the harbingers of the populist right, with statisticians and economists chief among the
various 'experts' that were ostensibly rejected by voters in
2016. Not only are statistics viewed by many as untrustworthy, there appears to be something almost insulting or
arrogant about them. Reducing social and economic issues
to numerical aggregates and averages seems to violate some
people's sense of political decency.

Nowhere is this more vividly manifest than with immigration. The think-tank British Future has studied how best
to win arguments in favour of immigration and multiculturalism. One of their main findings is that people often
respond warmly to qualitative evidence, such as the stories
of individual migrants and photographs of diverse communities. But statistics – especially regarding the alleged
benefits of migration to Britain's economy – elicit quite
the opposite reaction. People assume that the numbers are
manipulated and dislike the elitist nature of resorting to
quantitative evidence. Presented with official estimates of
how many immigrants are in the country illegally, a common response is to scoff. Far from increasing support for
immigration, British Future found, pointing to its positive
effect on GDP can actually make people more hostile to
it. GDP itself has come to seem like a Trojan Horse for an
elitist liberal agenda. Sensing this, politicians have largely
abandoned discussing immigration in economic terms.

All of this presents a serious challenge for liberal democracy. Put bluntly, the British Government – its officials,
experts, advisers and many of its politicians – *does* believe
that immigration is on balance good for the economy. The

British Government *did* believe that Brexit was the wrong choice. The problem is that the government is now engaged in self-censorship, for fear of provoking people further. This is an unwelcome dilemma. Either the state continues to make claims that it believes to be valid, but is accused by sceptics of propaganda. Or politicians and officials are confined to saying what feels plausible and intuitively true, but may ultimately be inaccurate. Either way, politics becomes mired in accusations of lies and cover-ups.

The declining authority of statistics – and of the experts who analyse them – is at the heart of the crisis that has become known as 'post-truth' politics. And in this uncertain new world, attitudes towards quantitative expertise have become increasingly polarised. From one perspective, grounding politics in statistics is elitist, undemocratic and oblivious to people's emotional investments in their community and nation. It is just one more way in which privileged people in London, Washington DC or Brussels seek to impose their worldview on everybody else. From the opposite perspective, statistics are quite the opposite of elitist. They enable journalists, citizens and politicians to discuss society as a whole, not on the basis of anecdote, sentiment or prejudice, but in ways that can be validated. The alternative to quantitative expertise is less likely to be democracy than an unleashing of tabloid editors and demagogues providing their own 'truth' about what's going on across society.

Is there a way out of this polarisation? Must we simply choose between a politics of facts and one of emotions, or is there another way of looking at the situation? One way is to relate statistics back to their history. We need to try to see them for what they are: neither unquestionable truths *nor* elite conspiracies, but tools designed to simplify the job of government, for better or worse. Viewed historically, we can see what a crucial role statistics have played in our understanding of nation states and their progress. This raises the alarming question of how – if at all – we will continue to have common ideas of society and collective progress should statistics fall by the wayside.

In the second half of the seventeenth century, in the aftermath of prolonged and bloody conflicts, European rulers adopted an entirely new perspective on the task of government, focused upon demographic trends – a perspective made possible by the birth of modern statistics. Since ancient times, censuses had been used to track population size, but these were costly and laborious to carry out, and focused on citizens who were considered politically important (property-owning men), rather than society as a whole. Statistics offered something quite different, transforming the nature of politics in the process.

One aspect of their novelty consisted in the aspiration to know a population in its entirety, rather than simply to pinpoint strategically valuable sources of power and wealth. In the early days, this didn't always involve producing numbers. In Germany, for example (from where we get the term *Statistik*), the challenge was to map disparate customs, institutions and laws across an empire of hundreds of micro-states. What characterised this knowledge as statistical was its holistic nature: it aimed to produce a picture of the nation as a whole. Statistics would do for populations what cartography did for territory. Equally significant was the inspiration of the natural sciences. Thanks to standardised measures and mathematical techniques, statistical knowledge could be presented as objective, in much the same way as astronomy. Inspired by Francis Bacon, pioneering English demographers such as William Petty and John Graunt adapted mathematical techniques to estimate population changes, for which they were hired by Oliver Cromwell and Charles II.

The emergence in the late seventeenth century of government advisers claiming scientific authority, rather than political or military acumen, represents the origins of the 'expert' culture now so reviled by populists. These path-breaking individuals were neither pure scholars nor government officials, but hovered somewhere between the two. They were enthusiastic amateurs who offered a new perspective on populations that privileged aggregates and objective facts. Thanks to their mathematical prowess, they believed they could calculate what would otherwise require a vast census to discover.

There was initially only one client for this type of expertise, and the clue is in the word 'statistics'. Only centralised nation *states* had the capacity to collect data across large populations in a standardised fashion, and only states had any need for such data in the first place. Over the second half of the eighteenth century, European states began to collect more statistics of the sort that would appear familiar to us today. Casting an eye over national populations, states became focused upon a range of quantities: births, deaths, baptisms, marriages, harvests, imports, exports, price fluctuations. Things that would previously have been registered locally and variously at parish level became aggregated at a national level.

New techniques were developed to represent these indicators, which exploited both the vertical and horizontal dimensions of the page, laying out data in matrices and tables, just as merchants had done with the development of standardised book-keeping techniques in the late fifteenth century. Organising numbers into rows and columns offered a powerful new way of displaying the attributes of a given society. Large, complex issues could now be surveyed simply by scanning the data laid out geometrically across a single page.

These innovations carried extraordinary potential for governments. By simplifying diverse populations down to specific indicators, and displaying them in suitable tables, governments could circumvent the need to acquire detailed local and historical insight. Of course, viewed from a different perspective, this blindness to local cultural variability is precisely what makes statistics vulgar and potentially offensive. Regardless of whether a given nation had any common cultural identity, statisticians would assume some standard uniformity or, some might argue, impose one on it.

Not every aspect of a given population can be captured by statistics. There is always an implicit choice in what is included and what is excluded, and this choice can become a political issue in its own right. The fact that GDP only captures the value of paid work, thereby excluding the work traditionally done by women in the domestic sphere, has made it a target of feminist critique since the 1960s. In France, it has been illegal to collect census data on ethnicity since 1978, on the basis that such data could be used for racist political purposes. (This has the side-effect of making systemic racism in the labour market much harder to quantify.)

Despite these criticisms, the aspiration to depict a society in its entirety, and to do so in an objective fashion, has meant that various progressive ideals have been attached to statistics. The image of statistics as a cool, objective science of society is only one part of the story. The other part is about how powerful political ideals became invested in these techniques: ideals of 'evidence-based policy', rationality, progress and nationhood grounded in facts, rather than in romanticised memories.

Since the high-point of the Enlightenment in the late eighteenth century, liberals and republicans have had great hopes that national measurement frameworks could produce a more rational politics, organised around demonstrable improvements in social and economic life. The great theorist of nationalism, Benedict Anderson, famously described nations as 'imagined communities', but statistics offer to anchor this imagination in something tangible.[10] Equally, they promise to reveal what historical path the nation is on – what kind of progress is occurring? How rapidly? For Enlightenment liberals, who saw nations as moving in a single historical direction, this question was crucial. The potential of statistics to reveal the state of the nation was seized in post-Revolutionary France. The Jacobin state set about imposing a whole new framework of national measurement and national data collection. The world's first official bureau of statistics was opened in Paris in 1800.

Uniformity of data collection, overseen by a centralised cadre of highly educated experts, was an integral part of the ideal of a centrally governed republic, which sought to establish a unified, egalitarian society.

From the Enlightenment onwards, statistics played an increasingly important role in the public sphere, informing debate in the media and providing social movements with evidence they could use. Over time, the production and analysis of such data became less dominated by the state. Academic social scientists began to analyse data for their own purposes, often entirely unconnected to government policy goals. By the late nineteenth century, reformers such as Charles Booth in London and W. E. B. Du Bois in Philadelphia were conducting their own surveys to understand urban poverty.

To recognise how statistics have been entangled in notions of national progress, consider the case of GDP. GDP is an estimate of the sum total of a nation's consumer spending, government spending, investments and trade balance (exports minus imports), which is represented in a single number. This is fiendishly difficult to get right. In the 1930s, efforts to calculate this figure began, like so many mathematical techniques, as a matter of marginal, somewhat nerdish interest. It was only elevated to a matter of national political urgency by the Second World War, when wartime governments needed to know whether the national population was producing enough to keep up the war effort. In the decades that followed, this single indicator, though never without its critics, took on a hallowed political status, as the ultimate barometer of a government's competence.

Whether GDP is rising or falling is now virtually a proxy for whether society is moving forwards or backwards.

Or take the example of opinion polling, an early instance of statistical innovation occurring in the private sector. During the 1920s, statisticians developed methods for identifying a *representative* sample of survey respondents, so as to glean the attitudes of the public as a whole. This breakthrough, which was first seized upon by market researchers, soon led to the birth of the opinion polling. This new industry immediately became the object of public and political fascination, as the media reported on what it told us about what 'women' or 'Americans' or 'manual labourers' thought about the world.

Nowadays, the flaws of polling are endlessly picked apart. But this is partly due to the tremendous hopes that have been invested in polling since its origins in the 1930s. Only to the extent that we believe in mass democracy are we fascinated or concerned by what the public thinks. But for the most part it is thanks to statistics, and not to democratic institutions as such, that we can know what the public thinks about specific issues. We underestimate how much of our sense of 'the public interest' is rooted in expert calculation, as opposed to democratic institutions.

As indicators of health, prosperity, equality, opinion and quality of life have come to tell us who we are collectively and whether things are getting better or worse, politicians have leaned heavily on statistics to buttress their authority. Often, they lean *too* heavily, stretching evidence too far, interpreting data too loosely, in the service of their cause. But that's an inevitable hazard of the prevalence of numbers in public life, and needn't necessarily trigger the type of wholehearted rejections of expertise that we've witnessed recently.

In many ways, the contemporary populist attack on expertise is born out of the same resentment as the attack on elected representatives. In talking of society *as a whole*, in seeking to govern the economy *as a whole*, both politicians and technocrats are believed to have 'lost touch' with how it feels to be a single citizen *in particular*. Both statisticians and politicians have fallen into the trap of 'seeing like a state', to use a phrase from the anarchist political thinker James C. Scott. Speaking scientifically about the nation – for instance in terms of macroeconomics – is an insult to those who would prefer to rely on memory and narrative for their sense of nationhood, and are sick of being told that their 'imagined community' does not exist. On the other hand, statistics (together with elected representatives) performed an adequate job of supporting a credible public discourse for decades if not centuries. What changed?

Origins of the current crisis

The crisis of statistics is not quite as sudden as it might seem. For roughly 350 years, the great achievement of statisticians has been to reduce the complexity and fluidity of national populations into manageable, comprehensible facts and figures. Yet in recent decades, the world has changed dramatically thanks to the cultural politics that emerged in the 1960s and the reshaping of the global economy that began soon after, and it is not clear that the statisticians have always kept pace with these changes. Traditional forms of statistical classification and definition are being strained by more fluid identities, attitudes and economic pathways. Efforts to represent demographic, social and economic changes in terms of simple, well-recognised indicators are losing legitimacy.

Consider the changing political and economic geography of nation states over the past forty years. The statistics that dominate political debate are largely national in character: poverty levels, unemployment, GDP, net migration and so on. But the geography of capitalism has been pulling in somewhat different directions. Plainly globalisation has not rendered geography irrelevant. In many cases it has made the location of economic activity far *more* important, exacerbating the inequality between successful locations (such as London or San Francisco) and less successful locations (such as North East England or the American Rust Belt). But the key geographic units involved are no longer nation states. Rather, it is cities, regions or individual urban neighbourhoods that are rising and falling.

The Enlightenment ideal of the nation as a single community, bound together by a common measurement framework, is becoming harder and harder to sustain. If you're living in a town in the Welsh Valleys that was once dependent on steel manufacturing or mining for jobs, politicians' talk about how 'the economy' is 'doing well' is likely to breed additional resentment. From that perspective, the term 'GDP' simply doesn't capture anything meaningful or credible.

When macroeconomics is used to make a political argument, this implies that the losses in one part of the country are more than offset by gains somewhere else. Headline-grabbing national indicators, such as GDP and inflation, conceal all sorts of localised gains and losses that are less commonly discussed by national politicians. Immigration may be good for the economy *overall*, but this doesn't mean that there aren't any local costs at all. So when politicians use national indicators to make their case, they implicitly assume some spirit of patriotic mutual sacrifice on the part of voters: you might be the loser on this occasion, but next time you might be the beneficiary. But what if the tables are never turned? What if the same city or region wins over and over again, while others always lose? On what principle of give-and-take is that justified?

In Europe, the currency union has exacerbated this problem. The indicators that matter to the European Central Bank (ECB), for example, are those representing half a billion people. The ECB is concerned with the inflation or unemployment rate across the eurozone as if it were a single homogeneous territory, at the same time as the economic fate of European citizens is splintering in different directions, depending on which region, city or neighbourhood they happen to live in. Official knowledge becomes ever more abstracted from lived experience, until that knowledge simply ceases to be relevant or credible any longer.

The privileging of the nation as the natural scale of analysis is one of the inbuilt biases of statistics that years of economic change have eaten away at. Another inbuilt bias that is coming under increasing strain is classification. Part of the job of statisticians is to classify people by putting them into a range of boxes that the statistician has created: employed or unemployed, married or unmarried, pro-Europe or anti-Europe. So long as people can be placed into categories in this way, it becomes possible to discern how far a given classification extends across the population. This can involve somewhat reductive choices. To count as unemployed, for example, a person has to report to a survey that they are *involuntarily* out of work, even if it may be more complicated than that in reality. Many people move in and out of work all the time, for reasons that might have as much to do with health and family needs as labour market conditions. But thanks to this simplification, it becomes possible to identify the rate of unemployment across the population as a whole.

But what if many of the defining questions of our age are answerable not in terms of the extent of people encompassed but in terms of the *intensity* with which people are affected? Unemployment is one example. The fact that Britain got through the 'Great Recession' of 2008–13 without unemployment substantially rising is generally viewed as a positive achievement. But the focus on 'unemployment' masked the rise of *under*-employment, that is, people not getting a sufficient amount of work or being employed at a level below that which they're qualified for. This currently accounts for around 6 per cent of the 'employed' labour force. Then there is the rise of the self-employed workforce, where the divide between 'employed' and 'involuntarily unemployed' makes little sense.

This is not a criticism of Britain's Office for National Statistics, which does now produce data on under-employment. But so long as politicians continue to deflect criticism by pointing to the unemployment rate, the experiences of those struggling to get enough work or to live off their wages go unrepresented in public debate. It wouldn't be all that surprising if these same people became suspicious of policy experts and the use of statistics in political debate, given the mismatch between what politicians say about the labour market and the lived reality.

The rise of identity politics since the 1960s has put additional strain on such systems of classification. Statistical data is only credible if people will accept the limited range of demographic categories on offer, categories which are selected by the expert not the respondent. But where identity becomes a political issue, people demand to define themselves on their own terms, whether in relation to gender, sexuality, race or class. Opinion polling may be suffering for similar reasons. Polls have traditionally captured people's attitudes and preferences on the reasonable assumption that people will behave accordingly. But in an age of declining political participation, it's not enough simply to know which box someone would prefer to put an 'X' in. One also needs to know whether they feel strongly enough about doing so to bother. When it comes to capturing such fluctuations in emotional intensity, polling is a clumsy tool.

The discipline of statistics has regularly faced criticism throughout its long history. The challenges that identity politics and globalisation present to it are not all that new either. Why then do the events of the last year feel quite so damaging to the ideal of quantitative expertise and its role in political debate? One reason is that an alternative to statistics is emerging that threatens to render many traditional forms of expertise redundant.

In recent years, a new way of quantifying and visualising populations has emerged that potentially pushes statistics to the margins, ushering in a different era altogether. Statistics, collected and compiled by technical experts, are giving way to data that accumulates by default, as a consequence of sweeping digitisation. Traditionally, statisticians have known which questions they wanted to ask regarding which population, then set out to answer them. By contrast, data is automatically produced whenever we swipe a loyalty card, comment on Facebook or search for something on Google. As our cities, cars, homes and household objects become digitally connected, the amount of data we leave in our trail will grow even greater. In this new world, data is captured first, research questions come later.

In the long term, the implications of this will likely be as profound as the invention of statistics was in the late seventeenth century. The rise of 'big data' provides far greater opportunities for quantitative analysis than any amount of polling or statistical modelling. But it is not just the quantity of data that is different. It represents an entirely different type of knowledge, accompanied by a new mode of expertise.

First, there is no fixed scale of analysis (such as the nation), nor are there any settled categories (such as 'unemployed'). These vast new data sets can be mined in search of patterns, trends, correlations and emergent moods, which becomes a way of tracking the identities people bestow upon themselves (via hashtags and tags) rather than imposing classifications on them. This is a form of aggregation suitable to a more fluid political age, in which not everything can be reliably referred back to some Enlightenment ideal of the nation state as guardian of the public interest.

Second, the majority of us are entirely oblivious to what all this data is saying about us, either individually or collectively. There is no equivalent of an Office for National Statistics for commercially collected 'big data'. We live in an age where our feelings, identities and affiliations can be tracked and analysed with unprecedented speed and sensitivity – but there is nothing that anchors this new capacity in the public interest or public debate. There are data analysts who work for Google and Facebook, but they are not 'experts' of the sort who generate statistics and who are now so widely condemned. Indeed, the anonymity and secrecy of the new analysts potentially makes them far more politically powerful than any social scientist.

A company like Facebook has the capacity to carry out quantitative social science research on hundreds of millions of people, at very low cost. But it has very little incentive to reveal the results. In 2014, when Facebook researchers published results of a study of 'emotional contagion' that they'd carried out on their users – in which they altered news feeds to see how it affected the content that users then shared in response – there was an outcry that people were being unwittingly experimented on. So, from Facebook's point of view, why go to all the hassle of publishing? Why not just do the study and keep quiet?

What is most politically significant about this shift from a logic of statistics to one of data is how comfortably it sits with the rise of populism. Populist leaders can heap scorn upon traditional 'experts', such as economists and pollsters, while trusting in a different form of numerical analysis altogether. Such politicians rely on a new, less visible elite, who seek out patterns from vast data banks, but rarely make any public pronouncements, let alone publish any evidence. These data analysts are often physicists or mathematicians, whose skills are not developed for the study of society at all. But this is consistent with the worldview propagated by, for example, Dominic Cummings, who has argued that 'physics, mathematics, and computer science are domains in which there are real experts, unlike macro-economic forecasting'.

Few social findings arising from data analytics ever end up in the public domain. This means that it does very little to help anchor political narrative in any shared reality. With the authority of statistics waning, and nothing stepping into the public sphere to replace it, people can live in whatever 'imagined community' they feel most aligned to and willing to believe in, which may or may not be a national one. Where statistics can be used to correct faulty claims about the economy, society or the population, data analytics does little to prevent people from giving way to their instinctive perspectives or emotional prejudices. On the contrary, companies such as Cambridge Analytica treat those feelings as things to be tracked.

But even if there were an 'Office for Data Analytics', acting on behalf of the public and the government as the ONS does, it's not clear that it would offer the kind of scientific perspective that liberals today are struggling to defend. The new apparatus of number-crunching is well suited to detecting trends, sensing the mood and spotting things as they bubble up. It serves campaign managers and marketers very well. It is less well suited to making the kinds of unambiguous, objective, potentially consensus-forming claims about society that statisticians and economists are paid for.

In this new technical and political climate, it will fall to the new digital elite to identify the facts, projections and truth amid the rushing stream of data that results. Whether indicators like 'GDP' and 'unemployment' continue to carry political clout remains to be seen, but if they don't, it won't necessarily herald the end of experts, still less the end of truth. The question to be taken more seriously, now that numbers are being constantly generated behind our backs and beyond our knowledge, is where the crisis of statistics leaves representative democracy.

On the one hand, it is worth recognising the capacity of long-standing political institutions to fight back. Just as 'sharing economy' platforms such as Uber and Airbnb have recently been thwarted by legal rulings (Uber being compelled to recognise drivers as employees, Airbnb being banned altogether by some municipal authorities), privacy and human rights law represents a potential obstacle to the extension of data analytics. What is less clear is how the benefits of digital analytics might ever be offered to the public, in the way that many statistical data sets are. Bodies such as the Open Data Institute, founded by Tim Berners-Lee among others, campaign to make data publicly available, but have little leverage over the corporations where so much of our data now accumulates. Statistics began life as a tool through which the state could view society, but gradually developed into something that academics, civic reformers and businesses had a stake in. But for many data analytics firms, secrecy surrounding methods and sources of data is a competitive advantage that they won't give up voluntarily.

A 'post-statistical' society is a potentially frightening proposition, not because it would lack any forms of truth or expertise altogether, but because it would drastically privatise them. Statistics are one of many pillars of liberalism, indeed of Enlightenment. The experts who produce and use them have become painted as arrogant and oblivious to the emotional and local dimensions of politics. No doubt there are ways in which data collection could be adapted to reflect lived experiences better. But the battle that will need to be waged in the long term is not between an elite-led politics of facts versus a populist politics of feeling. It is between those still committed to public knowledge and public argument, and those who profit from the ongoing disintegration of those things.

Theresa May's 'Protective State'

Over the course of 2014–15, I took part in a research project prompted by the government-sponsored campaign of 2013, when Theresa May was home secretary, in which vans carried billboards bearing the words 'In the UK illegally? Go home or face arrest.'[11] In order to understand how such a thing as that billboard could have come about, we felt we needed some insight into the mindset of the Home Office and its officials. One of the things we did was to talk, off the record, with various civil servants past and present.

In those conversations, a powerful image emerged of a department that had been embattled for a long time. In an era in which national borders were viewed as an unwelcome check on the freedom of capital and (to a lesser extent) labour, and geographic mobility was regarded as a crucial factor in promoting productivity and GDP growth, the Home Office, with its obsession with 'citizenship' and security, was an irritant to the Treasury and the Department for Business, Innovation and Skills. There has been an ideological conflict in Whitehall for some time regarding the proper relationship between the state, markets and citizens, but it has been masked by the authority of a succession of prominent, ambitious chancellors pushing primarily economic visions of Britain's place in the world. One can imagine the resentment that must have brewed among home secretaries and Home Office officials continually represented as the thorn in the side of Britain's 'economic competitiveness'.

The Home Office occupies a particular position vis-à-vis the public, which sometimes translates into class politics. Home secretaries are often moved by the plight of the defenceless in society: vulnerable children, elderly people plagued by rowdy teenagers on their estates, the victims of Harold Shipman (whose suicide apparently tempted David Blunkett to 'open a bottle'). Often, these people are defenceless because they are powerless, and they are powerless because they are poor, less well educated and culturally marginalised. And yet they are still British, and deserving of the state's defence. One former Home Office official told me that the Home Office has long been identified as the voice of the working class inside Whitehall, and feels looked down on by the Oxbridge elite in Downing Street and the Treasury. This person compared the ethos of the Home Office to that of Millwall fans: 'No one likes us, we don't care.'

Home secretaries see the world in Hobbesian terms, as a dangerous and frightening place, in which vulnerable people are robbed, murdered and blown up, and these things happen because the state has failed them. What's worse, lawyers and *Guardian* readers – who are rarely the victims of these crimes – then criticise the state for trying harder to protect the public through surveillance and policing.

I suspect that many home secretaries have developed some of these ways of thinking, including – or maybe especially – Labour home secretaries. Blunkett and John Reid certainly did. But Theresa May's long tenure (six years) and apparent comfort at the Home Office suggests that the mindset may have deepened in her case or meshed better with her pre-existing worldview. This includes a powerful resentment towards the Treasury, George Osborne in particular (whom she allegedly sacked with the words 'Go away and learn some emotional intelligence'), and the 'Balliol men' who have traditionally worked there. In making sense of May's extraordinary leader's speech at the 2016 Conservative Party Conference, the first thing to do is to put it back in the context of her political experience. For her, the first duty of the state is to protect, as Hobbes argued in 1651, and this comes before questions of 'left' and 'right'.

The 'protective state' May outlined was a state that looks after people. This is very different from the neoliberal state, whose job was characterised by Peter Mandelson, Bill Clinton and other Third Wayers in the 1990s as 'steering not rowing'. The target political audience of the neoliberal politician was always the 'hard-working family'. This imaginary unit had 'aspiration' and wanted to 'get ahead'. The state's job was to keep interest rates low on the assumption that people wanted to own assets, and otherwise to maintain a 'level playing field' so they could reap the rewards of all that hard work. Clearly most people cannot be conceived of as entrepreneurs in a neoliberal society – though the 'sharing economy' is now belatedly pressing that Thatcherite dream more deeply into the fabric of society – but they are assumed to be exerting themselves in order to become something better: richer, happier, healthier and so on. They are optimisers, just as economists assume in their models.

May has replaced 'hard-working families' with 'ordinary people', which includes the 'working class'. She says she wants the Tories to be the party of 'working people', though it no longer sounds as if these people are looking for much improvement or change in their lives. Faced with the unknown, they are more likely to retreat than found a start-up. They need looking after. This means that the necessities of life – health, energy, housing – must remain affordable, and threats must be kept at bay. The role of the state is not to initiate or facilitate change, but to prevent it, on the assumption that in general it is likely to be undesirable. Of course, in an age of political and economic crises, the 'protective state' must develop a very clear idea of who is to be looked after and who is to be rebuffed.

The state that looks after people (its own people) is not quite the same as the state that cares for people, of the sort that was developed in Britain after the Second World War.

If May wanted to push care to the centre of her vision, a new politics of welfare would be required, one which used fiscal policy to respond to basic material and social needs, where 'needs' are understood as things we all have by virtue of our humanity, not our identity. A care-oriented state would have to pursue a far-reaching cultural reversal of the Osbornite condemnation of welfare recipients. There were some signs, during the early months of May's premiership, that the more punitive end of recent welfare policies would be abandoned. It will be interesting to see how much more of that there is to come. But for the time being, it sounds as if the May government is going to listen to the fears and demands of its particular people, rather than seek to map and meet the needs of people in general.

Economic liberals are already nervous that the new prime minister is a protectionist. Outside her Home Office brief, there are signs that her thinking – and that of her policy adviser, Nick Timothy – departs from the neoliberal consensus in key ways. Abandoning Osborne's austerity targets and declaring war on tax evaders are signs that the financial sector and the very wealthy can no longer view the Conservative Party as their tool. Timothy's vision of 'Erdington conservatism' (named after the working-class area of Birmingham where he grew up) imagines the state intervening in the economy to defend the interests of the immobile against the mobile – protecting 'ordinary' parents, patients and workers, who are too often left dependent on slack services and callous bosses, and cannot simply up sticks and go elsewhere. In that way of seeing things, this is something liberals and the wealthy will never understand because they've probably never experienced hardship. Resonances with Blue Labour and Red Toryism – communitarian policy movements that emerged after 2008 with the aim of challenging economic and social liberalism at the same time – have been widely noted.

There is no contradiction between social conservatism and economic protectionism: both are hostile to the fluidity, cosmopolitanism and perceived snobbery of liberalism. May's conference declaration, 'If you believe you're a citizen of the world, you are a citizen of nowhere', was pitched as much at bankers as it was at left-wing intellectuals. Whether it was also a 'dog-whistle' regarding refugees probably depends on what breed of dog you are. I was surprised that a speech condemning financial elites, human rights lawyers and nationless people in blanket terms wasn't interpreted as antisemitic. But as Stuart Hall recognised, rampant capitalism has a far greater capacity to undermine traditional community relations than social liberalism: the Thatcherite effort to weld social conservatism to economic liberalism was far more contradictory than the present turn to economic interventionism. This latest reconfiguration of conservatism could ultimately be more sustainable even than Thatcher's.

We currently have no idea what May's actual intentions are in this respect, just as we have no very clear idea of how actively she would like to police the boundaries of 'British citizenship'. In all likelihood, the two agendas – the economic and the nationalist – will emerge in tandem: there was a hint of this in the new home secretary Amber Rudd's suggestion that companies be forced to list their foreign workers. Prejudice in society carries far more potential when it is also pursued in the economy. The reason German neoliberals (or 'ordoliberals') of the 1930s and 1940s were so hostile to cartels and monopolies wasn't that they saw them as necessarily inefficient, but that non-market economies can be more easily requisitioned in the service of political goals: they were a vital precondition of the Nazi political economy. By contrast, competitive markets perform a liberal function, because they block the social and political ambitions of interventionist leaders. I am not suggesting any direct analogy here, but if neoliberalism is indeed now giving way to a new political-economic formation, we should be alert to the various new social and cultural opportunities this offers the state, and not only those that pertain to the economy. Protectionism (of indigenous industries and workers) is never simply an economic policy, but involves clear statements of who is in and who is out.

The European Union was founded partly on ordoliberal principles, which require the state to provide a rigid legal constitution in defence of open and competitive markets; hence the inclusion of anti-trust and anti-state aid provisions in the Treaty of Rome. Member states are simply not allowed to 'pick winners' and defend 'national champions' or look after those who have greater claims to indigenous economic rights (though the application of these rules has been variable, and states have always wanted to do favours for their nation's leading car manufacturers). This European post-nationalism is what Brexit was pitted against. May and Timothy have far greater legal and political opportunity to pursue a protectionist agenda now that Britain is on its way out of that ordoliberal framework. If May was a secret

Brexiteer, that might be why. The question is the extent to which Britain's withdrawal will cause any of the ordoliberals' grave fears to be realised, in Britain or on the Continent, should the basic competitive framework of the EU start to be dismantled.

Britain is now a more unequal society than it has ever been since the Second World War. Class is a powerful determinant of the lives people lead. It doesn't, however, perform quite the same role in sustaining the cultural and political status quo that it did before neoliberalism, and certainly not the same role it did before the 1960s, which helps to explain why May's 'protective state' has become possible and necessary. One thing that Brexit demonstrated, which May is clearly keen to exploit, is that cultural divisions no longer map tidily onto economic ones. Working-class lives are buffeted by change, including the changes represented by immigration, but New Labour only ever invited people to embrace more change. The traditional middle classes and aristocracy have not been in the driving seat of British politics for more than thirty years, as the financial elite exploited the exuberance of *fin de siècle* Britain, London especially. It's been said that Thatcher wanted a society of people like her father, but produced a society of people like her son.

Clearly May wants to change that. But the new cultural coalition that she aims to represent – of working-class Brexiteers, pensioners, *Daily Mail* readers and traditionalists – scarcely holds together as an identifiable group. Nor are the boundaries around these identities very clear cut. They may well aggregate into a fearful electoral resource, but it is quite another thing for the state actively to intervene to look after these people, when historically it was the job of cultural institutions, ties, networks and communities to preserve their way of life. May's cultural instincts are consistent with Burkean conservative philosophy, but that tradition is historically uncomfortable with state intervention of the sort she espoused in her party conference speech. To wed a Burkean ideal of community to a Hobbesian ideal of the protective state is problematic and potentially dangerous. The difficulty for Burkean conservatives today is that neo-liberalism destroyed the resources on which 'little platoons' depend and thrive, so that tacitly understood conventions and rituals must now be reintroduced by the very thing that conservatives traditionally wanted to avoid depending on – namely, the modern state. The gaping hole in the Blue Labour and Red Tory agendas was always the question of statecraft: what exactly will the state do to promote the ideal of 'faith, flag and family'?

It seems likely that the state will start performing acts of conservative discrimination which historically have been performed by way of cultural capital and softer forms of power. An example of how deranged the consequences can be is Nick Timothy's suggestion that work visas be granted only to foreign students at Oxbridge and Russell Group universities. Policymakers may form their ideas on the basis of what goes down well in the pubs of Dorset, the comment pages of the *Daily Mail* or the working men's clubs of Scarborough, but snobbery and chippiness are more troubling when they are converted into the printed word of the statute book.

It sounds as if the 'protective state' is ready to discriminate, and won't be ashamed to admit it. It will discriminate regarding good and bad economic activity; it will discriminate between good and bad migrants; it will discriminate between good and bad ways of life. May is not afraid of sorting the wheat from the chaff. This may be the reason grammar schools symbolise something important for her, regardless of the evidence against their efficacy. In that respect, there is some continuity with neoliberalism, which sought to divide 'winners' from 'losers' in a range of different tests and competitive arenas. The key difference is that neoliberalism uses rivalry itself to identify the worthy. The neoliberal state offers no view on what a good company or school or artist looks like. Instead, it uses rankings, contests and markets in order to find out who rises to the top. The question any neoliberal – or liberal for that matter – might now want to ask May is this: on what basis do you distinguish the worthy from the unworthy? Are we now simply to be driven by the contingency of biography, where Timothy is fuelled by the anger he felt as a lower-middle-class boy in Erdington in the early 1990s, or May is guided by the example of her Anglican clergyman father? Is the fact that liberals haven't experienced being the victim of regular petty crime or a failing school now going to be the principal basis for ignoring them?

Politicians have always used cultural tropes in order to build popularity and even hegemony. Thatcher spoke a nationalist, militarist language, while doing considerable harm to many of Britain's institutions and traditions. Blair had his football, coffee mug and badly fitting jeans.

Conservatives have often struggled to find a coherent post-Blair cultural scheme, alternating between fake displays of liberalism (Cameron's huskies) and the embarrassing reality of their party base. Right now, however, matters of nationality and cultural tradition do not seem like window-dressing: when the state is offering to look after some of us, but not all of us, the way you look, talk, behave and learn threatens to become the most important political issue of all.

'Strong and Stable'

Britain today confronts a variety of deep, even existential, uncertainties. The terms of its exit from the European Union, the country's long-term economic prospects and Scotland's future within the United Kingdom are all in the balance. In contrast to these unknowns, the outcome of the forthcoming general election already feels concrete: the Conservatives, consistently between 17 per cent and 20 per cent ahead in the polls, are on course for a landslide victory. In calling this election (despite promises not to) and in her campaigning for it, Prime Minister Theresa May is exploiting this contrast. The Conservatives are being presented as a new type of 'people's party', under which everyone can huddle to stay safe from the multiple storms that are brewing. Mrs May and her party are treating this election as too important to be reduced to political divides. With no explanation of how, she claims that 'every single vote for me and Conservative candidates will be a vote that strengthens my hand in the negotiations for Brexit'.

This is where May's strategy and rhetoric become

disconcerting. Ever since she took over from David Cameron last summer, she has spoken as if Britain is a nation harmoniously united, aside from the divisive forces of party politics and liberal elites seeking to thwart the 'will of the people'. The first part of this is simply untrue: 48 per cent of the public voted to remain in the European Union, while the other 52 per cent held various ideas of what leaving could or should mean in practice.

May's idea that her opponents are merely playing self-interested political 'games' is a classic populist trope, one that suggests that constitutional democracy is really an obstacle standing between people and leader. The prime minister's rhetoric since calling the general election has implied that the best outcome for 'the national interest' would be to eradicate opposition altogether, whether that be in the news media, Parliament or the judiciary. For various reasons (not least the rise of the Scottish National Party), it is virtually impossible to imagine the Labour Party achieving a parliamentary majority ever again, as May well knows. To put all this another way, the main purpose of this election is to destroy two-party politics as Britain has known it since 1945.

One way in which May has aggressively pursued this outcome is in her unusual framing of the choice before the British electorate. We are used to politicians presenting policy proposals and promises to the public. Of course, in practice this involves spin doctors seeking to cast their party's policies in the best light, news outlets twisting the message depending on their political biases, and many voters turning away in disgust because they don't believe a word politicians say. That's the routine. The Labour Party, despite occasional populist swipes at the news media, has been sticking roughly to this script. There is a certain irony in this, seeing as Labour, under the socialist leadership of Jeremy Corbyn, has become viewed by many pundits and voters as an implausible party of government. But Labour has nevertheless been regularly putting out clear and reasonably worked-out policy proposals since the election was announced on 18 April.

By contrast, May has made scarcely any statements regarding policy. Her speeches and campaign literature are peppered with the slogan 'strong and stable leadership', a phrase she then recites on the few occasions that she takes questions from journalists or members of the public. The very basis on which she is asking to be trusted and to be elected seems different from an ordinary policy platform. From a leader of a party still in thrall to Margaret Thatcher, May's virtual silence on the economy is astonishing. The decision to vote Conservative is not to be based on knowledge of what a Conservative government will do – nobody has much of a clue about anything right now – but because of the desperate need for 'strong and stable leadership'.

Symbolically and rhetorically, May's campaign message is simple and potentially overpowering. While opposition parties dirty their hands with policy ideas and news conferences, she is seeking to personify the nation state itself – a job that technically belongs to the Queen. In one of her campaign videos, which sees her speaking solemnly in front of a Union Jack in a dimly lit room as if announcing a new war, she uses the term 'us' in multiple ways: at times it means the Conservative Party, at others it means the government, and at other times it means Britain itself. The mesmerising effect on the viewer is to lose track of the differences among the three. Representative democracy is being denigrated as petty and harmful to the national interest by a woman who has just called an unnecessary and unwanted election.

Where does this leave the opposition? The fear is that outside of Scotland, rival political parties will be reduced to the status of glorified think-tanks or non-governmental organisations. If they come up with good ideas, May's government can happily adopt them. Already, the Conservatives have picked up one popular Labour Party policy for controlling the retail price of energy. With the Conservatives branded as more than just a political party, it is hard to see how their electoral stranglehold over England and Wales will be broken.

Politicians and parties can scarcely be blamed for wanting more power. That's what drives them. What is worrying about May is that she seems to be deliberately aggravating Britain's existential anxiety, precisely so as to benefit from it personally. Her extraordinary Trumpian accusation that European Union leaders are seeking to interfere in the election (since repeated by other Conservative ministers) seems to be aimed at stoking nationalist resentment towards the very people who will end up deciding what type of trade deals and 'divorce bill' Britain will be granted.[12] This suggests that she views the destruction of the Labour Party as a more important national priority than Britain's long-term economic prosperity.

Even if May is democratically successful in channelling

the fears and resentments of what she calls 'ordinary working people', she will still face fearsome political obstacles. If it turns out that she is a weak negotiator with the European Union, and if she fails to grasp the magnitude of Britain's economic vulnerability, the politics of resentment will be all she has to fall back on. Britain's conservative tabloid press will praise every step in this direction with its usual wartime nostalgia, and she will continue to claim the support of 'the people'. But the reality will be a fractured nation slipping ungraciously to the status of an angry and irrelevant mid-size economy.

Brexit will be fiendishly difficult, but there is no reason it has to be draped in so much nationalistic gravitas and secrecy, nor does it have to mean the hugely risky departure from the European single market. But that's the path that Mrs May has chosen. Her gambit is to present herself and the Conservative Party as the one certainty in an otherwise chaotic political situation, with party politics a symptom of weakness and chaos. This is likely to work to devastating effect, but only because she refuses to acknowledge the crucial contribution that she and her party made to this chaos in the first place.

2
Quagmire

Theresa May's fateful decision to call an early general election, resulting in the shock of a hung Parliament and the high watermark for Corbynism, exposed aspects of conservative and Brexit ideology that otherwise might have been concealed. The election campaign, followed quickly by Grenfell, and then the Windrush scandal of the following year, trashed May's communitarian image. The sudden weakening of her leadership meant that she was no longer able to contain or control the forces of nationalism that were becoming increasingly vocal within her own party and its sympathetic newspapers. These forces would spend the rest of her premiership pushing for an ever harder, more punitive type of Brexit, no matter how much economic or political harm it did in the process. Crucially, May failed to exude the necessary mood of the hard Brexiteer, choosing instead to focus on detail, process and policy, where the demand was for something irresponsible and brash. With the foundation of Farage's Brexit Party in late 2018, and the looming recognition that May would have to extend Britain's membership of the

EU beyond March 2019, the limits of her strategy were made abundantly clear.

The Corbyn Shock

When the internet first became part of everyday life in the late 1990s, it was celebrated as a wondrous new publishing machine, an amalgam of printing press and broadcaster that would radically democratise the means of communication at virtually zero cost. As any blogger or YouTube star can confirm, this dream didn't die altogether, but neither did it capture what would turn out to be a more distinctive characteristic of the emerging technology. Twenty years on, it has become clear that the internet is less significant as a means of publishing than as a means of archiving. More and more of our behaviour is being captured and stored, from the trace we leave in online searches, the photos we share and 'like' on social media platforms to the vast archive of emails and tweets to which we contribute day after day. This massive quantity of information sits there, ready to be interpreted, if only something coherent can be extracted from the fog. It makes possible a new, panoramic way of assessing people, now that evidence of their character can be retrieved from the past – a fact that hasn't escaped consumer credit rating firms or government border agencies.

YouTube, Spotify, Google Books and so on put decades' worth, sometimes centuries' worth, of 'content' at our fingertips. One effect of this is the compression of historical time. 'Is it *really* fifty years since *Sergeant Pepper*?' you may ask. But the time lapse feels immaterial. The internet turns up a perpetual series of anniversaries, disparate moments from disparate epochs, and presents them all as equivalent and accessible in the here and now. 'In 1981,' Mark Fisher wrote in *Ghosts of My Life*, 'the 1960s seemed much further away than they do today.'[1] Facebook extends this logic to people's own personal history, informing them of what banal activity they were engaged in this time last year, or eight years ago. The archive isn't merely available to us; it actively pursues us.

These phenomena have extended well beyond the limits of any particular digital platform, producing a more diffuse cultural logic. This is manifest in the novels of Karl Ove Knausgaard, or Richard Linklater's film *Boyhood*, where the 'big data' mentality of capturing every biographical detail over time is elevated to an artform. This cultural epoch introduces a distinct set of problems. Which event from the past will pop up next? How can a clear narrative be extracted from the deluge of messages and numbers? What does my data trail say about me? Can past judgements of oneself or others be revised or revoked? It can seem as if there are only two options: to immerse oneself entirely, or to not give a damn. The figures who succeed in today's populist politics are the ones who don't give a damn. Politicians in the past may have sought 'authenticity', but that use of the term was always oxymoronic. If you're trying too hard, you're not authentic. When politics was still oriented around analogue television and newspapers, there were specific audiences for politicians' performances and well-defined opportunities for them to exercise their charm: the TV debate, the interview, the press conference, their relationships with newspaper editors. But now that politicians (like the rest of us) are subject to ceaseless, wide-ranging monitoring, and leave a mountainous archive of evidence behind them, focal points of the traditional sort don't matter so much. It will all come out anyway.

It is also telling that these successful populists are significantly older than your average 1990s 'Third Way' politician. Where the latter was a man in his early forties (now re-enacted by Emmanuel Macron), in recent years we have witnessed the unforeseen rise of Bernie Sanders, Jeremy Corbyn and Donald Trump, the oldest man ever to become president. These men have lurked on the margins of public life for decades, and a stockpile of images and stories has accumulated around them. Both Corbyn and Sanders have an impressive archive, appearing in photographs as young men being manhandled by police as they protested against racial segregation. It isn't just their words that persuade people they offer a break from the status quo, their biographies do too. They have accrued the political equivalent of rich credit histories.

One event that did a great deal to push the 'big data' sensibility into UK politics, yet had little to do with the internet (it was triggered by a newspaper freedom of information request), was the MPs' expenses scandal of 2009. Its significance for our subsequent democratic upheavals hasn't been fully appreciated. The capacity to peer into our representatives' lives, find out what curtains they bought, whether they take taxis or the tube, where they go for lunch, circumvented the staged performances on which politicians prefer to be judged. It revealed differences of character and taste, the sort of thing we're now used to glimpsing via Facebook or Instagram.

Thanks to the tabloids, we have long been accustomed to the interruption of politics by scandal, including stories designed to cause the greatest possible personal embarrassment. But here was something different. In place of the revelation of David Mellor's bedroom attire came a drip-drip of inane yet telling details of purchases from John Lewis, which didn't interrupt politics as usual so much as reconfigure it altogether. That Ed Miliband was revealed as the most frugal member of the cabinet, and his brother one of the most extravagant, spoke of something more important than their views on fiscal policy, and whatever that was seeped into the Labour leadership contest the following year.

One of the striking results of this new media ecology is that traditional smears no longer seem to work as effectively as they once did. Both Hillary Clinton in 2016 and Theresa May in 2017 sought to do down their opponents by drawing attention to their past behaviour. A tape of Trump bragging about grabbing women 'by the pussy' was leaked, presumably on the assumption that it would finish off his campaign once and for all. Corbyn was hammered over and over again for his past sympathies with the IRA, with the effect that Labour's manifesto (and its vulnerabilities on Brexit) went relatively untouched.

The strategy failed because in this new environment, there is something worse than to err, and that is to be two-faced. Trump's behaviour was shocking but scarcely out of character. Aggression and an overturning of 'political correctness' were what fuelled his campaign in the first place. As for Corbyn, his entire political career has been spent challenging Western imperialism and military rule. These smears didn't tell the public much that they hadn't already sensed – and could find out by Googling – about the candidates' characters and priorities. By contrast, 'liberal elites' are vulnerable to the charge that their public and private lives don't match up: they preach public service and altruism, while having two kitchens (Ed Miliband), making $675,000 from speeches to Goldman Sachs (Clinton) or not knowing exactly how many properties they own (David Cameron).

Hannah Arendt remarked in *On Violence* that rage is less commonly provoked by injustice than by hypocrisy. The difficulty is that politics *must* involve some degree of hypocrisy, if public and private life aren't to dissolve into each other. 'Be the change you wish to see in the world' is a useful ethical heuristic, but it doesn't help judges, civil servants or ministers in taking decisions on behalf of the public. It won't help Corbyn either if he becomes prime minister, despite his protestations that he would continue to maintain his allotment from Downing Street. Yet in many ways digital media serve to dissolve the division between public and private, allowing a relentless, unforgiving gaze to be cast on every discrepancy between words and actions, words past and words present. In the gladiatorial world of Twitter, the greatest mistake one can make isn't to be offensive (that can be a virtue) but to contradict an earlier tweet, sometimes even from years ago, which can then be gleefully dug up again by trolls. Under these conditions, public credibility depends on boundless sincerity and obsessive consistency, as well as a disregard for the way one is seen by others. Trump's archive does him few favours here: his back catalogue of tweets provides a constant source of entertainment in exposing the hypocrisy of his behaviour as president, though primarily for those who never believed him in the first place. This flies in the face of Machiavellian tenets concerning political prowess, which helps explain why non-politicians, marginal politicians and non-parties are now reaping the electoral benefits.

Given the degree to which conventional notions of leadership had become shaped to suit television and newspapers, the challenge to these notions is long overdue. Silly staged performances of normality must be finished for the time being. What was heartening about the 2017 general election was that it suggested a new symbolic status for policy of the sort that technocratic politics was unable to manufacture. Amid all the noise, slogans and smears of the campaign, it seems that Labour's simple, eye-catching policies (free university tuition, more bank holidays, free school meals for all, more NHS funding, no tax rises for 95 per cent of earners) had the ability to cut through. These policies were crafted to produce a left-populist platform, with the idea in mind that policies can influence voters, but only if they are sufficiently straightforward to be able to hold their shape as they travel around an increasingly complex, chaotic public sphere. New Labour had two sets of experts: one to run its technocratic policymaking machine, the other to handle the media, which it believed could be tamed. But once editorial bottlenecks no longer determine the flow of news, and neurotic control of image is no longer realistic, policies must be designed to spread of their own accord, like internet memes. Trump's 'Build a wall!' did this. Less propitiously for the Tories, once the phrase 'dementia tax' had attached itself to their campaign, it couldn't be dislodged.

This isn't to say that Corbyn himself wasn't instrumental. Given the surge in youth turn-out, 'free university tuition' may have been decisive in ruining May's hopes of a majority, especially given Corbyn's promise to explore ways of alleviating existing debt burdens. But not just any leader could credibly have made this promise: Nick Clegg famously reneged on it in 2010, and no Clegg-alike could have got away with making it in 2017. Centrist Labour figures and their friends in the press continue to believe it is a bad policy, on the grounds that it uses general taxation to subsidise middle-class privileges. Corbyn is different, not because he has a different view of the economics, but because he has a different political biography. What's more, he has become a valuable asset in the 'attention economy' of the digital landscape, as eyes are drawn inexorably towards personal and emotional quirks. As with Trump during his election campaign, Corbyn converted weaknesses into strength. The combination of his avuncular demeanour and the earnest policy-heavy document of the Labour manifesto proved an unexpected hit.

Blairites complain that Corbyn offers simple solutions to complex problems. But one of Corbyn's solutions is difficult to argue with – namely, the resurrection of fiscal policy as a central tool of social and economic transformation, following twenty-five years in which both parties were paranoid about being tagged as 'tax and spend' fanatics. For the last ten years central bankers have pleaded with politicians to use fiscal policy more liberally in order to relieve the macroeconomic burden on monetary policy, but their call has fallen on deaf ears, especially in Europe. Coming in the wake of quantitative easing, one of the most technically obscure economic policies ever devised, the return of fiscal policy is welcome, both economically and politically. Corbyn has forced the Conservatives' hand on this, turning austerity into a toxic political issue.

During the 1980s and 1990s, theorists such as Fredric Jameson argued that capitalism had brought about a fundamental change in the way cultural and political history are experienced. The distinctively modern sense of chronology, which emerged in the second half of the nineteenth century, viewed the past as unfolding progressively into the present, and the future as a space of new political and cultural possibilities to be seized by whichever artist, planner or political movement was bold enough. Postmodernity, by contrast, involved a collapse of historical progress into a perpetual present, a constant rehashing and recombining of existing styles and ideas, which put an end to any hope (or fear) that the future might be radically different.

The economic corollary of this was the entrenching of a neoliberal order in which liberal capitalism was treated as the final stage of human history: the only plausible plans were business plans, the only source of innovation was entrepreneurship. This vision still held on to some notion of progress, but it was now tightly bound to improvements in economic efficiency and consumer experiences. When Tony Blair used the word 'modernisation', he meant driving competition into public services. The idea of the 'modern' was shorn of its utopian or politically disruptive implications, provoking the suggestion that the future no longer existed, at least not as something different from the present.

The years of austerity since the global financial crisis have followed the postmodern script, but with one crucial difference. Postmodernity is typically conceived as repetitive, but playfully so. By contrast, austerity has come to be experienced as an endless, pointless repetition of pain (Yanis Varoufakis described Greece's bailout conditions as 'fiscal waterboarding'). With each announcement that austerity will have to be extended because spending cuts have failed once more to reduce the government deficit (just as most economists warned all along they would), the sense of disbelief has grown. In the worst cases, such as Greece, deficit-reduction schemes extend decades into the future. Precarity and rising housing costs trap young people in a state of perpetual pre-adulthood, unable to separate themselves from their parents. The need to escape this loop is ever more pressing, yet all that governments have been promising is more and more of it.

In these circumstances, hope is found in a form of historical revisionism. The successes of Corbyn and Sanders (and, in a different way, Trump) allow us to feel that it might be possible to restore and re-evaluate elements of a past which predates neoliberalism. Where the modernist's view of history would treat the march of Reagan, Thatcher, Blair and Clinton as a necessary stage en route to something better, the current sense seems to be that theirs was a path taken in error. Instead, we must go back to go forward. In the case of Trump, the perceived error goes back much further, to the 1964 Civil Rights Act and before. What is notable about Trump's brand of conservatism is that it shows little devotion to Reagan or recent conservative history, seeking instead to imagine away much of postwar US history in favour of a hologram of a nation where men manufacture the world's goods and women iron their shirts.

A large part of the reason Corbyn causes Blairites so much distress – whether or not they dislike his policies or style of leadership – is that he threatens to destroy their narrative about the 1980s and 1990s. In that version of history, the hard left was heroically defeated by Neil Kinnock, setting the stage for the most successful Labour Government ever. What if Corbyn were to win a general election? How would that recast the significance of those battles? The coincidence of the Corbyn surge with the horror of Grenfell Tower has created the conditions – and the demand – for a kind of truth and reconciliation commission on forty years of neoliberalism. It is too simple to cast Corbyn as a throwback, but it is undeniable that his appeal and his authority derive partly from his willingness to cast a different, less forgiving light on recent history, so that we don't have to carry on repeating it.

Reacting to the breakdown of the vote on 8 June, business leaders and conservative commentators have expressed their disquiet at the fact that young people are so enthusiastic about an apparently retrograde left-wing programme. 'Memo to anyone under 45', Digby Jones, the former director general of the CBI, tweeted: 'You can't remember last time socialists got control of the cookie jar: everything

nationalised & nothing worked.' To which the rebuke might
be made: and you don't remember how good things were
compared to today. Speak to my undergraduate students
about the 1970s and early 1980s, and you'll see the wistful
look on their faces as they imagine a society in which art-
ists, writers and recent graduates could live independently
in Central London, unharassed by student loan companies,
workfare contractors or debt collectors. This may be a
partial historical view, but it responds to what younger generations are currently cheated of: the opportunity to grow
into adulthood without having their entire future mapped
out as a financial strategy. A leader who can build a bridge
to that past offers the hope of a different future.

The Riddle of Tory Brexitism

When historians examine Britain's departure from the
European Union, one of the things that will puzzle them is
the behaviour of the Conservative Party. Thanks to copious
demographic and geographical analysis, we are already
in a position to make sense of the 2016 referendum result
itself. But it remains difficult to grasp how the Tories could
effectively have taken what was to everyone else a fringe
issue and used it to attack the interests they had until very
recently represented: the City of London, big business, the
Union, even Whitehall.

To paraphrase Neil Kinnock, how did we end up in the
grotesque chaos of a Conservative government – a *Conservative* government – setting about the seemingly deliberate
demolition of the United Kingdom and its economy? From

a Tory perspective, things must have reached a sorry pass when the sole voice speaking up for the Union belongs to Arlene Foster, leader of the Democratic Unionist Party. However much energy the Leave campaign put into stirring up nationalist and anti-immigration sentiment, it is hard to see the Westminster Brexiteers as nationalists when they show so little regard for the integrity of the UK or its governing institutions. If the economic forecasts are remotely accurate, Brexit will render England, let alone the United Kingdom of Great Britain and Northern Ireland, a hoax nation. The most regionally imbalanced nation in Europe will become even more so, as the North suffers yet further decline while the South East holds on. Much of South Wales and Northern Ireland will exist in a parallel economic universe to London.

What do they want, these Brexiteers? The fantasies of hardliners such as Daniel Hannan and Jacob Rees-Mogg are based on dimly learned lessons from British history. The mantra of 'Global Britain' resurrects an ideal of laissez-faire from the era of Manchester cotton mills and New World slavery. Discussing the range of Brexit options at a Tory conference fringe event in October, the former Brexit minister David Jones concluded: 'If necessary, as Churchill once said, very well then, alone.' This is the sort of nostalgia Stuart Hall warned against as early as the 1970s, and which Peter Ammon, the outgoing German ambassador in London, identified recently when he complained that Britain was investing in a vision of national isolation that Churchill had played up (and vastly exaggerated) in his wartime rhetoric.[2]

Do they even believe the myth, or is it an expedient way of bashing opponents while pursuing some ulterior goal? Historical re-enactment may be fine for the *Daily Mail* and the grassroots, but it doesn't seem a strong enough motivation to support a professional political career. We need to know not just what kind of past the Brexiteers imagine, but what kind of future they are after. One disconcerting possibility is that figures such as Hannan and Rees-Mogg might be willing to believe the dismal economic forecasts, but look on them as an attraction.

This isn't as implausible as it may sound. Since the 1960s, conservatism has been defined partly by a greater willingness to inflict harm, especially in the English-speaking world. The logic is that the augmentation of the postwar welfare state by the moral pluralism of the 1960s produced an acute problem of 'moral hazard', whereby benign policies ended up being taken for granted and abused. Once people believe things can be had for free and take pleasure in abundance, there is a risk of idleness and hedonism. In the United States, this fear was expressed in the cultural conservatism of the Nixon era, during which moral opprobrium was visited on welfare claimants and feckless liberals. The focus was on race and gender: in the conservative imaginary, compassion would be exploited in the economic realm by black women, and in the judicial realm by black men. In Britain, there was more emphasis on the language of economics, specifically the 'supply side' idea that the interests of investors and entrepreneurs were paramount. As the theory behind Thatcherism had it, government services shrink everybody's incentives to produce, compete and invest. They reduce the motivation for businesses to deliver services, and ordinary people's desire to work. Toughness, even pain, performs an important moral and psychological function in pushing people to come up with solutions.

This style of thinking drove Thatcher through the vicious recession of the early 1980s. It was encapsulated by Norman Tebbit in his conference speech in 1981, often misquoted: 'I grew up in the 1930s with an unemployed father. He didn't riot. He got on his bike and looked for work, and he kept looking till he found it.' That would imply that economic hardship should produce a more mobile population, and perhaps further abandonment of deindustrialised regions. A more interventionist version of such thinking appeared with the development of 'workfare' programmes by the Clinton and Blair governments of the 1990s, which sought to repurpose the welfare state as a means of boosting claimants' 'employability' as well as their efforts to find work. Under workfare schemes, benefits were either paid to those already in work in the form of 'tax credits', or made conditional on enrolment in training programmes and constant job-hunting. The old British idea of the 'dole' (or in America of 'welfare'), as something that was an alternative to work, was quickly eradicated. And there was a new iteration under David Cameron and George Osborne, in the form of austerity. The hypothesis of 'expansionary fiscal contraction', touted by Osbornites during the first years of the Coalition Government, is that cuts to public spending *can* lead to economic growth, by creating more opportunities for the private sector to invest. As most economists predicted, the hypothesis turned out to be false, but thanks partly to the workfare policies left behind by New Labour, levels of unemployment under austerity didn't reach those of the Thatcher recession, and Theresa May's government achieved the lowest unemployment rate since the mid-1970s. An alternative perspective on that achievement is that hardship has forced people into worse jobs, demanding fewer skills and lower capital investment, so that Britain's productivity growth has stalled to a degree not seen since the Industrial Revolution. That is what happens when work is framed as a moral duty, to be engaged in at all costs.

The fear of 'moral hazard' produces a punitive approach to debtors, be they households, firms or national governments, the assumption being that anything short of harshness will produce a downward spiral of generosity, forgiveness and free-riding, eventually making the market economy unviable. Osborne liked to claim (against all the evidence coming from the bond markets) that if Britain kept borrowing, lenders would lose trust in the moral rectitude of the government and interest rates would rise. Gratification must be resisted. Pain *works*. Only pain forces people to adapt and innovate. In practice that may mean all sorts of things: migrating, reskilling, sacrificing weekends or family time, selling property, the 'gig economy' and so on. The productiveness of pain is a central conservative belief, whose expression might be economic, but whose logic is deeply moralistic.

There seems little doubt that for many of Thatcher's followers the free market experiment hasn't gone far enough. As long as there is an NHS, a welfare state and a public sector that is more European than American in scale, we will never truly discover what the British people are made of, because they will never be forced to find out. Steve Bannon, the former Trump strategist, has often voiced the opinion that America's only hope of moral cleansing lies in war. Tory Brexiteers tend not to go that far, but they may well be holding out for a milder version of the same idea, an extreme of economic hardship that means government is no longer capable of picking up the pieces. No wonder families in County Durham or the Welsh Valleys have experienced multiple generations of unemployment, they argue: there's been adequate unemployment benefit. The estimated £80 billion hit to the public finances caused by Brexit might change that. And that's before we take up the suggestive comment lurking in the official forecasts that 'leaving the European Union could provide the UK with an opportunity to regulate differently across social, environmental, energy, consumer and product standards'.[3]

The optimistic version of this story is that it's only when the chips are down that we discover what people are truly capable of. Brexit might reveal reserves of courage and innovation that have lain dormant for decades, held back by the interferences of bureaucracy and public spending. And if it doesn't? Well, then the truth is laid bare. Perhaps that will be the moment for a more heroic form of political leadership to rise from the ashes. Several prominent Tory Brexiteers, including Iain Duncan Smith and Steve Baker, have military backgrounds. As with the Second World War, Brexit will perform an X-ray of our collective moral fibre. Remainers love facts, but are afraid of the truth.

This is, I suspect, as close to a Conservative ideology of

Brexit as exists. At the very least, it has some internal coherence, whatever it may lack in detail regarding the future. But we shouldn't exaggerate the coherence of Tory Brexit. The situation is a mess, one aspect of which is the frightening lack of responsibility displayed by its main instigators. The political weather in Westminster has been made over the past two years by Boris Johnson, a man whose only apparent goal is to make the political weather. Senior Leave campaigners, such as Dominic Cummings, admit they would have lost the referendum had Johnson not leaped on board. He approaches public life as a game in which he commits sackable offences as a way of demonstrating his unsackability. The office of foreign secretary in this administration is treated as a leash to constrain someone who would otherwise cause more trouble to the prime minister elsewhere.

Johnson is as close as British politics has to a Trump problem, and his seniority suggests that Trumpism has permeated our political culture more deeply than we like to admit. Trump may be a more acute case, but both men compel all around them to react to their idle remarks, mistakes and fantasies. On the day President Macron visited Britain, to take just one recent example, Johnson declared that he wanted to build a bridge across the Channel, and that became the headline. Trump and Johnson are 'real-time' politicians: they dominate the rolling news cycle, and devalue the painstaking aspect of politics in the process. Psychologically, they are inverses: Trump has no sense of humour, where Johnson sees the funny side of everything. Johnson is said to strut around Whitehall asking civil servants if they've found his £350 million a week yet: 'I know it exists because it was written on my bus.' Ha ha. No doubt men such as Johnson and Trump have always existed, but healthy political systems have ways of keeping them away from the highest echelons of power.

For all his idiosyncrasies, Johnson typifies something about contemporary conservatism, which might best be understood biographically. The cultural forces shaping the new conservatism resolve in a particular stereotype: men born between the mid-1960s and the early 1970s, with some constellation of expat backgrounds, famous fathers and first careers in the media. All four things apply to Johnson, but a Venn diagram of these various characteristics would also include Michael Gove, Douglas Carswell, Daniel Hannan and Jacob Rees-Mogg. The result of these disparate characteristics is a comfortable familiarity with the myths and rituals of the British State, but a blasé indifference to the impact of policy. The expat perspective seems to play an important role in the psychology of Brexit. Hannan and Carswell both had expatriate childhoods. Astute observers have argued that Brexit rests more on an imperial imaginary than on a national one. But as much as anything the expat is in a position to see 'Great Britain' from a perspective other than that of government. Such things as statistics, macroeconomics and policy itself fade into insignificance compared to the way the nation is seen from afar, alongside its historical rivals. Ignore 'official Treasury forecasts' and focus on the atlas instead.

In contrast to the populist message of UKIP, which is all about British blood, British soil and how the elites have betrayed them, Tory Brexitism can have a strange flippancy about it. In some cases, you wonder if they really mean it or if it's just another attention-seeking strategy. Like Johnson, Rees-Mogg was treated as a joke until suddenly he was being discussed as a potential Conservative leader. Then there are their allies who write in the *Spectator* and specialise in exploring the sliver of political space between irony and bigotry. Among them is Toby Young, who originally found fame as the butt of his own joke with his memoir *How to Lose Friends and Alienate People*. The game is a quest for attention, and humorous transgression is the key skill in winning it. Another name for it is 'trolling'.

Armchair psychoanalysts can muse on what responsibility the high-profile fathers of these men have for cultivating their sons' delinquency and need for attention. It is surely a safer psychological force confined to op-ed pages than unleashed on politics, especially where historic constitutional reform is at stake. But the boundary separating the conservative press from the Conservative Party has in any case been slowly dissolving, with the *Times* (Gove's former employer, which currently boasts two Conservative peers, Lords Finkelstein and Ridley, on its comment team) occupying a particularly porous position on the border between the two. In January 2018, Young came within a Twitter-storm of being appointed to the new Office for Students, which will regulate universities in England and Wales. The reality is that in addition to the ideological and cultural forces behind Brexit, it is also happening thanks to the recklessness of individuals who see public life as an opportunity to show off. This is the more fundamental sense in which Westminster is being permeated by Trumpism.

These men's contemporaries on the centre-left had the existential fortune of beginning their careers in tandem with Blairism. The likes of Ed Balls, David Miliband and Andy Burnham threw themselves into the details of policy design and implementation, with a level of technocratic commitment that would eventually provoke populist derision from both left and right. No doubt this clique contained some planet-sized egos too, but one thing that can be said for the New Labour generation is that they saw politics as a serious business, requiring hard, serious work. Among Tory Brexiteers, by contrast, ignorance and a lack of effort is taken almost as a mark of distinction – how else to explain David Davis? Having spent so long witnessing the Blairite policy machine churn out evidence and evaluations, year after year, with impeccable economic logic, it's as if they have abandoned such dull, humourless pursuits altogether. Hence their disdain for the Treasury and for the man, 'Spreadsheet Phil' Hammond, who runs it.

In his book *Propaganda*, published in 1928, Edward Bernays, the creator of modern public relations (and Sigmund Freud's nephew), expressed his optimism that expert communication strategies could protect democracy from the psychological excesses of mass society (it is sometimes forgotten that Bernays saw 'propaganda' as a positive and civilising force). Modern democracy would have to draw on the most advanced techniques of communication and persuasion, just as modern business had done with advertising, if the masses were to be satisfied with the policies and leaders that were available.

Bernays believed that politicians struggle to understand

the importance of communication strategy, because they never have to struggle hard enough to win public attention. Unlike businesses, which have to work hard to attract publicity, political parties and politicians get attention from the media regardless of how well thought-out their message is. Bernays believed there was a risk that mass democracies would come undone unless politicians gave more thought to how they presented themselves in the media. Recent history suggests that he was worrying about the wrong thing. The professionalisation of politics and the rise of spin led to the opposite problem: politicians began to think too carefully about how they presented themselves in the media. The image management of the Blair and Clinton era smacked of inauthenticity, a charge that was later levelled at mainstream political parties in general, leading to the populist upheavals of the past few years.

But there is a further risk lurking in Bernays's analysis, which he seemingly didn't anticipate. If professional politicians have an unearned advantage over others when it comes to attracting public attention, there is a danger that politics comes to attract people who only want public attention – such as Johnson – and others who only know how to exploit it, such as Rees-Mogg. While Rees-Mogg may be a firm believer in the Victorian moral vision of Brexit, there can be no denying that his currently elevated status is largely down to the fact that he is recognisable and provides good media 'content'. When the media report his latest comments, it's because he is someone whom everyone recognises from the media. Everything he says or does must be calculated to ensure that this remains the case. As any troll understands, wit and disruption are the best tactics for succeeding in the 'attention economy'.

It would be almost reassuring to know that there was an ideology of Tory Brexit that was driving things, just as there is an ideology known as 'Lexit' which views the EU as an anti-democratic neoliberal institution that must be resisted. But for the generation who entered public life in the 1990s, after the 'end of ideology', there were only two choices: to devote oneself with immense earnestness to the nitty-gritty of policy and economics, or to revel in the freedom of symbolism and storytelling, as journalists, PR professionals and pranksters. Political careers came later. Britain's misfortune is that matters of the greatest seriousness are now in the hands of basically unserious people.

The Windrush Nightmare

'Someone must have been telling lies about Josef K.' We never find out whether or not the opening line of *The Trial* is true, or what the lies might have been. Instead we are led into a suffocating world of innuendo and gossip, which slowly builds towards a judicial decision that doesn't in the end arrive. Unable to discover what he's been accused of, Josef K. focuses on trying to navigate a system that is as senseless as it is cruel, ultimately without success. The world portrayed in *The Trial* is one in which judiciary and bureaucracy have collapsed into each other. The intimidating symbolism of the courtroom is married to the pettiness and absurdity of bureaucracy, creating a web that traps the book's hero for no clear reason. It isn't so much that he is suffering an injustice, as that he can barely work out what the justice system wants of him or how he might provide it. The real trial is the constant process, rather than the hearing itself.

It is difficult to imagine anything more Kafkaesque than the experience the 'Windrush generation' has undergone at the hands of the British state in the past few years. Cases are accumulating of people seeking NHS treatment, passports, jobs or housing only to find themselves having to prove their right to live in the country where they have been legally resident for more than forty-five years, or risk being deported. Harrowing stories have emerged of individuals being made homeless, jobless and stateless, after they failed to produce proof they were never given in the first place. One man suffered an aneurysm which he believes was brought on by the stress the situation caused him, only to be presented with a bill for £5,000 for his NHS treatment – again because his paperwork didn't measure up – while also losing his job and his home. He was left on the street. As it turns out, the one source of evidence that might have put a stop to this torture – the landing cards that recorded arrivals from the Caribbean until the 1960s – was destroyed by the Home Office in 2010.

The Windrush generation's immigration status should never have been in question, and the cause of their predicament is recent: the 2014 Immigration Act, which contained the flagship policies of the then home secretary, Theresa May. Foremost among them was the plan to create a 'hostile environment' that would make it harder for illegal immigrants to work and live in the UK. By forcing landlords, employers, banks and NHS services to run immigration status checks, the policy pushed the mentality of border control into everyday social and economic life. The 2016 Immigration Act extended it further, introducing tougher penalties for employers and landlords who fail to play their part in maintaining the 'hostile environment', and adding to the list of privileges that can be taken away from those who cannot prove their right to live and work in the UK.

Another key feature of the 2014 Act was that it empowered the Home Office to deport people more quickly and cheaply, avoiding lengthy and repeated appeals. The 'deport first, appeal later' provision was eventually ruled unlawful by the Supreme Court. The Act greatly restricted the right to appeal via tribunal, replacing most appeals with an administrative review carried out by the Home Office itself. Before the Act was introduced, 50 per cent of appeals were upheld at tribunal; at administrative review, the figure is 18 per cent.

Immigration policy necessarily involves complex alliances and tensions between legal and bureaucratic logic. People move across national borders for any number of reasons, and practicality (not to mention compassion) requires that these be recognised in a variety of different visas and entitlements. The Home Office is under constant pressure, not least from other parts of Whitehall, to recognise the needs of business, universities and the economy as a whole, and therefore to let valued migrants into the UK, at least for a period of time. The nature of Britain's economy and labour market means that immigration law cannot be cleanly separated from issues of employment, welfare, health and education. One of the dangers of the 'hostile environment' policy is that it deliberately collapses the distinction between judicial due process and bureaucratic administration. It's almost as if, on discovering that law alone was too blunt an instrument for deterring and excluding immigrants, May decided to weaponise paperwork instead. The 'hostile environment' strategy was never presented just as an effective way of identifying and deporting illegal immigrants: more important, it was intended as a way of destroying their ability to build normal lives. The hope, it seemed, was that people might decide that living in Britain wasn't worth the hassle.

The policy has echoes of the 'benefit sanctions' regime the Coalition Government introduced in 2012 to penalise 'jobseekers' who failed to meet specific conditions such as attending daily appointments at job centres. Claimants have had their income cut off at a moment's notice for reasons that were beyond their control: one man was sanctioned for nine weeks after having a heart attack on the day of his appointment. The thread linking benefit sanctions and the 'hostile environment' is that both are policies designed to alter behaviour dressed up as audits. Neither is really concerned with accumulating information per se: the idea is to use a process of constant auditing to punish and deter. If it seems senseless, that's the point (as Hannah Arendt wrote, 'To use reason when reason is used as a trap is not "rational"').[4] The Coalition Government was fond of the idea of 'nudges', interventions that seek to change behaviour by subtle manipulation of the way things look and feel, rather than through regulation. Nudgers celebrate the sunnier success stories, such as getting more people to recycle or to quit smoking, but it's easy to see how the same mentality might be applied in a more menacing way. Policies such as the creation of a 'hostile environment' work by cultivating anxiety among those they target, in tandem with campaigns such as the quickly aborted 'Go Home' vans introduced on Britain's streets in August 2013 in an effort to persuade illegal immigrants to hand themselves in.

One problem with governing via mood is that there is no precise way of controlling who you affect and how. It's no good saying that the innocent have nothing to fear: fear doesn't work like that. In any case, the argument for creating a 'hostile environment' rests on the assumption that legal and illegal residents are prima facie indistinguishable, and can only be separated through constant hounding. The Home Office's frustration with the courts is that they place the burden of proof on the state. The 2014 Act sought to shift it onto the individual. If, like members of the Windrush generation, you can't prove you are British, you become de facto illegal.

Another problem with governing via mood is that the effect of policy becomes a subjective matter. This is where racism comes in. The 'hostile environment' and associated campaigns don't have to be conceived and designed by racists in order to look, feel and be racist, especially given certain family resemblances between these policies and everyday racist practices of the past. Granting landlords additional powers to evict tenants who can't prove their legal status (as the 2016 Immigration Act did), or plastering the words 'Go Home' across a billboard, creates a sense of déjà vu.

The 'Go Home' vans, which were introduced along with a range of other Home Office information campaigns challenging the image of Britain (and its public services) as a soft touch, had two different audiences in mind. First, those it hoped to persuade to 'go home'. The Home Office can cover the cost of illegal immigrants leaving the country, and wanted to get the message out there. The problem was that May and her advisers feared this might look over-generous. They were more mindful of a second audience: the voters and the *Daily Mail*. This is what caused the messaging to be toughened up, until it (deliberately or otherwise) revived a notorious bit of racist graffiti from the 1970s.

The ultimate ambition of the Home Office in all of this is to reduce the number of people living illegally in the UK. Under May, it pursued this goal with a set of techniques designed to comfort a majority and frighten a minority. But whether an individual falls into the first or the second camp doesn't depend only on their legal status. It is also a matter of how settled and welcome they feel in the UK, not to mention their capacity to produce paperwork. Nobody has suffered from this policy as badly as the Windrush victims, but countless British citizens of colour will have seen pictures of the vans, been asked for additional paperwork by landlords (perhaps more often than their white counterparts), and wondered if, deep down, this country really wants them. The news of the past month will have deepened their anxiety.

Is the prime minister a racist? It's a provocative question that has been asked repeatedly since Home Office rhetoric on illegal immigration was ratcheted up around 2012.

Her 2016 party conference speech, containing its infamous dismissal of 'citizens of nowhere', raised the question once more. Lord Kerslake, head of the civil service between 2012 and 2014, has said that some inside the government saw May's immigration policies as 'almost reminiscent of Nazi Germany'. But reducing the current situation to the politics or prejudices of an individual doesn't really explain how Britain descended to the point where black citizens were being stripped of their dignity and livelihoods, and threatened with being slung out of the country. This isn't just a matter of something rotten in the Home Office, as Amber Rudd had the nerve to suggest. That we have ended up in this mess suggests that senior politicians have gradually lost all sense of proportion on the matter. Someone must have been telling lies about immigration.

The tabloid media are culpable, with their talk of 'floods' and 'swarms', happily echoed by Nigel Farage. But the most significant precursor to the 'hostile environment' was David Cameron's ill-fated pledge of 2010 to reduce net migration (the number entering the UK minus the number leaving) to less than 100,000 a year, at a time when the figure was more than 250,000. New Labour had treated immigration merely as a labour market issue, without much political significance. Cameron's policy was a desperate bid to hang on to voters who might drift towards UKIP, but it was wildly undeliverable. The government soon introduced a cap on the number of skilled non-EU migrants that could enter the country, which was broken month after month.

Between the Blair and May governments, the source of immigration changed substantially. Only 13 per cent of people entering Britain between 2000 and 2003 came from the European Union. By 2015, almost half were from the EU, which meant that the power of the Home Office to limit the number of arrivals was falling fast. Yet Cameron reiterated his pledge (downgraded to an 'ambition') at the 2015 election, by which point net migration was close to 300,000 a year. Cameron was backing himself to persuade the EU to make an exception for Britain in relation to free movement, which he could then use as the basis to win a referendum on EU membership. The first wager ended in farce and the second in tragedy.

What does any of this have to do with the 'hostile environment'? The net migration numbers obviously don't capture the number of people entering the country illegally in the backs of lorries. There is no data on how many people get into the country that way, though a pessimistic report by the think-tank Civitas put the number at 40,000 a year (based on figures from the summer of 2015 for the number being caught – at the time, 1,000 per month). While it is politically expedient for the Home Office to conjure images of criminals and people-trafficking when unveiling their latest crackdown, the people ensnared by the 'hostile environment' policy rarely fit this profile. Most will have entered the country legally for work, study or tourism, but outstayed their visa or abused its terms. Many will be honestly unsure of their exact status. Some of the rules are so complicated, and the financial cost of navigating them so high, that people are unable to discover or prove their status conclusively, no matter how hard they try.

In a politically desperate situation, with Cameron having

repeatedly pledged to deliver the impossible, May put forward two measures that would reduce the net migration rate. First, hounding people to provide paperwork at every turn would reduce the likelihood that immigrants would make a life for themselves in the UK. If you can't limit the number of people coming into the country legally, then maybe you can boost the number going out. Second, casting doubt on people's legal status: 'sham marriages', fake colleges and dodgy employers would be unmasked. The number of legal routes into the country can be restricted by exposing some of them as not so legal after all. The trademark Home Office suspicion that the law on its own is too generous and open to abuse has made it a matter of border enforcement to address such thorny questions as what constitutes a *real* marriage, or who is a *real* student. This is an area ripe for legal challenge and embarrassment, as doubt is cast on legitimate practices as well as less legitimate ones. In March 2016, a court ruled that the Home Office had behaved unlawfully in deporting thousands of foreign students accused of cheating in an English language test, when the only evidence against any of them was the confession of the firm that administered the test. The students, who were mostly Indian, had been rounded up in dawn raids and deported without the right to appeal.

In total, the Home Office manages to remove around 40,000 people from the UK every year, either forcibly or through 'voluntary departure' (what the 'Go Home' vans were ostensibly seeking to encourage). This number includes those who have got as far as a British airport or port, but have then been refused entry. No doubt the number

could go higher as additional hostility and extra-legal measures are threaded into civil society and the economy. As
the Windrush scandal unfolded, it emerged that the Home
Office has internal targets for the number of 'voluntary
departures', raising the pressure on its staff to track down
anyone whose documents aren't in perfect order. But at what
point will a home secretary place a cap on the level of fear
and paranoia they are willing to manufacture? The suffering
of the Windrush generation is not a result of administrative
'incompetence', as defenders of the 'hostile environment'
have argued. The system exists to harass people who are
trying to live ordinary, non-criminal lives.

Net migration will fall only when fewer people want to
come to the UK, and when universities, employers and the
tourist industry stop inviting them. Thanks to Brexit, the
first of these things is already happening: net migration
suddenly fell by a third in the year following the referendum. The worry is that if 'hostile environment' policies are
sustained after Brexit, they will start to affect EU citizens
who (like the Windrush generation) entered the country
with unambiguous rights, so never built up the paperwork
needed to document them.

There is nothing accidental about the grotesque events
that have befallen the Windrush generation. We need to ask
how public policy and administration became so warped as
to enact them. Not only has the politics become delusional,
nowhere more so than in the case of Cameron's pledge. Our
entire way of understanding and talking about migration
has gone awry. When home secretaries speak of 'illegal
immigrants', they mostly mean people who entered the

country legally. When they speak of 'borders', they often mean hospitals, homes, workplaces and register offices. As the experience of the twentieth century warned, when language stops working, all manner of things are possible.

The Revenge of Sovereignty on Government

'I am increasingly admiring of Donald Trump. I have become more and more convinced that there is method in his madness.' These comments, subsequently leaked, were made in June 2018 by Boris Johnson, who was then Britain's foreign secretary. Never one to discount praise, Trump reportedly expressed an interest in meeting his 'friend' Johnson during his subsequent visit to London, noting that Johnson has been 'very, very nice to me, very supportive'. When Johnson offered those remarks praising the American president, he was discussing the topic that shapes everything in British politics right now: Brexit. The dilemma that is pulling Prime Minister Theresa May's government apart, and may yet topple her, is whether Britain opts for a 'soft' Brexit, in which it leaves the European Union but retains many of its rules, or a 'hard' Brexit, which throws caution to the wind and releases Britain to start all its trading negotiations afresh. In Johnson's view, it seems, Trump would have no hesitation in choosing the latter. One thing the two men share is a recklessness that looks like courage in the eyes of their supporters, but which also sabotages the work of policymaking and diplomacy.

May's most recent attempt to escape the 'hard' versus 'soft' dilemma involves establishing a 'common rule book'

shared by London and Brussels. This looks far too 'soft'
for the liking of fervent Eurosceptics in her party. Within
forty-eight hours of the plan being revealed, Johnson had
resigned. Before him, so had David Davis, another prominent Brexiteer in May's cabinet who had been put in charge
of negotiating with the European Union. In characteristi-
cally florid terms, Johnson's resignation letter expressed
fears that 'we are headed for the status of a colony'.

Just to further destabilise an already fragile political situation, Trump's visit was accompanied by an incendiary
interview with the *Sun*.[5] Confirming Johnson's assess-
ment, while escalating the mutual admiration between the
two men, Trump declared that May's plan would 'kill' any
future trade deal between Britain and the United States, and
that Johnson would 'make a great prime minister'. On the
lengthy efforts of May's government to arrive at a compromise with Brussels, Trump scoffed that 'deals that take too
long are never good ones'.

Like so many political metaphors, the distinction between
'hard' and 'soft' is misleading. Any Brexiteer wanting to
perform machismo will reach for the 'hard' option. But
as has become increasingly plain over the past two years,
nobody has any idea what 'hard' Brexit actually means in
policy terms. It is not so much hard as *abstract*. 'Soft' Brexit
might sound weak or half-hearted, but it is also the only
policy proposal that might actually work. What appear on
the surface to be policy disputes over Britain's relationship
with Brussels are actually fundamental conflicts regarding
the very nature of political power. In this, the arguments
underway inside Britain's Conservative Party speak of a

deeper rift within liberal democracies today, which shows no sign of healing. In conceptual terms, this is a conflict between those who are sympathetic to government and those striving to reassert sovereignty.

When we speak of government, we refer to the various technical and bureaucratic means by which policies and plans are delivered. Government involves officials, data-gathering, regulating and evaluating. As a *governmental* issue, Brexit involves prosaic problems such as how to get trucks through ports. Sovereignty, on the other hand, is always an abstract notion of where power ultimately lies, albeit an abstraction that modern states depend on if they're to command obedience. As a *sovereign* issue, Brexit involves bravado appeals to 'the people' and 'the nation'. These are two incommensurable ideas of what power consists of, although any effective state must have both at its disposal.

One way to understand the rise of reactionary populism today is as the revenge of sovereignty on government. This is a backlash not simply against decades of globalisation, but against the form of political power that facilitated it, which is technocratic, multilateral and increasingly divorced from local identities. A common thread linking 'hard' Brexiteers to nationalists across the globe is that they resent the very idea of governing as a complex, modern, fact-based set of activities that requires technical expertise and permanent officials. Soon after entering the White House as President Trump's chief strategist, Steve Bannon expressed the hope that the newly appointed cabinet would achieve the 'deconstruction of the administrative state'. In Europe, the European Commission – which has copious governmental capacity, but scant sovereignty – is an obvious target for nationalists such as Prime Minister Viktor Orbán of Hungary.

The more extreme fringes of British conservatism have now reached the point that American conservatives first arrived at during the Clinton administration: they are seeking to undermine the very possibility of workable government. For hardliners such as Jacob Rees-Mogg, it is an article of faith that Britain's Treasury Department, the Bank of England and Downing Street itself are now conspiring to deny Britain its sovereignty. It is thought that David Davis's real grudge was with the unelected official, Olly Robbins, who had usurped him in his influence over the Brexit process. The problem was that Mr Robbins is willing and able to do the laborious and intellectually demanding policy work that Brexit will require, while Mr Davis is famously not.

What happens if sections of the news media, the political classes and the public insist that only sovereignty matters and that the complexities of governing are a lie invented by liberal elites? For one thing, it gives rise to celebrity populists, personified by Trump, whose inability to engage patiently or intelligently with policy issues makes it possible to sustain the fantasy that governing is simple. What Johnson terms the 'method' in Trump's 'madness' is a refusal to listen to inconvenient evidence, of the sort provided by officials and experts.

But another by-product of the anti-government attitude is a constant wave of exits. Britain leaves the European Union, Johnson resigns from the cabinet. The Trump White House has been defined by the constant churn of sackings and resignations. With astonishing hypocrisy, wealthy Brexiteers such as Rees-Mogg, John Redwood, Lord Lawson and Lord Ashcroft have all been discovered either preparing to move their own assets into European Union jurisdictions or advising clients on how to do so. No doubt when Britain does finally leave the European Union, they will distance themselves from reality once more, allowing the sense of victimhood and the dream of 'sovereignty' to live another day. Meanwhile, someone has to keep governing.

The Lure of Exit

It is received wisdom about referendums that 'yes' has an advantage over 'no'. Alex Salmond didn't get the wording he wanted for the 2014 Scottish independence referendum – the Electoral Commission considered 'Do you agree that Scotland should be an independent country?' too much of a leading question – but he did at least make sure that his side would be fighting for a 'yes'. The campaign to legalise abortion in Ireland, which won with a thumping 'yes' vote in last year's referendum, was a masterclass in positivity. Britain's EU referendum was not a matter of 'yes' or 'no'. Even so, the government may have reassured themselves that 'leave' carried more negative resonances than 'remain'. Leave ... and go where exactly? What kind of affirmation is *leave*? What kind of identity or vision does it assert? But among the many things unreckoned with by David Cameron's government, when it initiated Britain's current political disaster, was the extent to which voters were up for a bit of negativity.

The vote for Brexit was a 'no' to many things: wage stagnation, mass immigration, local government cuts, Brussels, London, Westminster, multiculturalism, 'political correctness' and who knows what else. Political scientists and pollsters can spend as much time as they like disentangling one factor from another in an effort to isolate the *really* decisive one, but Leave's greatest advantage was that it didn't have to specify exactly what was being left. As the *gilets jaunes* in France have shown, 'no' has the capacity to mobilise a more disparate movement than 'yes', without the need for any consensus on what is being negated. Leave was a coalition of rejecters, a great refusal that didn't require a positive or viable programme in order to flourish.

In his book *Down to Earth*, Bruno Latour spots a pattern in this instinct to leave that is far from unique to Britain. Underlying it, he thinks, is a fantasy of escape, ultimately from a shared planet that is becoming less habitable. 'We can understand nothing about the politics of the last fifty years', he writes, 'if we do not put the question of climate change and its denial front and centre.'[6] This isn't to say that all politics is now about carbon dioxide emissions, but that all politics is now terrestrial: there is a finite (and shrinking) amount of firm ground available, and the problem of how to share and conserve it is growing. As for Brexit, 'the country that had invented the wide-open space of the market on the sea as well as on land, the country that had ceaselessly pushed the European Union to be nothing but a huge shop; this very country, facing the sudden arrival of thousands of refugees, decided on impulse to stop playing the game of globalisation'.[7]

The British do not lack for people wanting to tell them

who they are. Whether these opinions have come from the most credible sources is doubtful. Too much attention has been paid to whiggish, conflictless tales of national identity and tradition, and not enough to the insights of those who stand one foot in, one foot out, in particular those with the ambivalent perspective of the once colonised. If it's never too late to learn, then there should be a rush to the works of Paul Gilroy on Britain's 'postcolonial melancholia', just as there is now an embrace of Fintan O'Toole's reflections on Britain's sudden sense of victimhood.

But even this will not bring us face to face with the sheer negativity of Brexit. In the ongoing struggle to make sense of what Brexit is and why it is happening, ample attention has been paid to the 'Br', but comparatively little to the 'exit'. The seductions, myths and affirmations of nationhood are raked through in search of what all this is about. Empire? Race? The Blitz? But what if the answer has been staring us in the face all along? What if there is in British political culture a deep, generalised urge to depart?

What is currently clear is that there is no majority support, either in Parliament or in the country, for the hard graft of actively withdrawing Britain from the European Union. The polls register a consistent lead for Remain in any future referendum on the question (in a YouGov poll on 6 January 2019, the lead was 46 to 39 per cent, with the other 15 per cent so alienated from the whole business that they offer no answer one way or the other). A sufficient number of Leave voters has now had enough of Brexit, or of politics in general, for Remain to stand a plausible chance of winning a second referendum.

Nor is there any conceivable parliamentary majority on the horizon that might support a tangible withdrawal agreement. The extraordinary scale of Theresa May's defeat on 15 January, by 230 votes, once again demonstrated the power of 'no'. The 432 MPs who voted against her did so for a variety of reasons, underpinned by incompatible visions of what should happen next. There are few things that could produce consensus between Jeremy Corbyn, Arlene Foster, Vince Cable and Jacob Rees-Mogg, but opposition to May's deal was one. Jean-Claude Juncker, the president of the European Commission, responded to the result with a tweet urging the UK 'to clarify its intentions as soon as possible'. But what if 'the UK' does not possess any intentions right now?

May's gambit, seen at first as a smart one, of putting leading Brexiteers in critical ministerial positions, has gradually disintegrated thanks to a steady stream of resignations. Boris Johnson's departure from the Foreign Office was the most eye-catching, but the successive exits of David Davis and Dominic Raab from the office of Brexit secretary conveyed a sense that theirs was an ideology that couldn't survive its own implementation. The committed Brexiteer knows only one tactic: exit, and when that doesn't work, exit again.

In his classic treatise from 1970, *Exit, Voice and Loyalty*, the economic theorist Albert Hirschman articulated the different ways power is exerted in the economy. In principle, competitive markets are systems in which 'exit' counts for everything. If I am unhappy with the quality of my washing powder, I can simply decline to buy it again, and choose a different brand in future. If enough consumers do the same, the manufacturer will eventually get the message, and either improve its product or get driven out of the market altogether. In a free market, exit is the default way of expressing oneself.

Hirschman realised that markets never quite match up to this ideal. Often, consumers will make a fuss (Hirschman called this 'voice'), reporting the problem, demanding a refund or – increasingly nowadays – leaving critical feedback. To take a key example, the relationship between employers and employees can't simply be abandoned at the first sign of difficulty: it involves negotiation, trust and occasional conflict. In short, there is always a space for politics, even where markets appear to have free rein. By studying the subtle interactions between 'exit' and 'voice', Hirschman was seeking to understand the entanglement of economics and politics, markets and democracy, in everyday life.

Much of the time, exit and voice are things we hold in reserve, as rights rather than everyday behaviours. Most consumers don't keep switching their brand of washing powder, any more than most voters continually harangue their MP with demands and complaints. But the point is that we retain the right to do these things, which grants us a modicum of power. And these rights have their own proper domains: exit in the market sphere, voice in the political sphere.

How did the ideology – or the fantasy – of exit engulf British politics? How did a principle that belongs in the marketplace, the principle of expressing dissatisfaction through departure, trigger the greatest constitutional crisis since 1945? Viewed this way, Brexit isn't so much a celebration of sovereignty or democracy, as a new frontier in the marketisation of politics. It is the fundamental right of any investor, customer or business to leave when it suits them – so why not nations too? As the armchair trade negotiators of the Conservative Party's European Research Group keep reminding us, you don't get a good deal on anything unless you're willing to walk away.

Hirschman noted that consumers or businessmen who become too accustomed to withdrawing can gradually forget how to assert themselves in any other way: 'The presence of the exit alternative can therefore tend to atrophy the development of the art of voice.'[8] Perhaps the inverse is true in the democratic arena: where the art of voice has atrophied too much, there is an increasing appetite for the exit alternative. This isn't to say that the European Commission has ever been very open to 'voice', least of all a popular one. One of Cameron's worst strategic errors in committing to a referendum in January 2013 was to promise a major unilateral renegotiation of Britain's EU membership, which Brussels was never going to accept.

But voice had been atrophying across British society for decades before 2016.[9] Trade union membership in the UK peaked at more than 50 per cent of the workforce in 1979, but has since declined to just 23 per cent. The mantra of 'choice' and 'competition' in public services, which was central to New Labour's modernisation programme, rested on the assumption that improvements could come about only once service users had powers of exit similar to the ones they had in the private sector. The turn-out in the 1992 general election was 78 per cent; nine years later, it was 59 per cent.

Developing alongside these trends was a new political common sense about globalisation and the rising mobility of capital, and of the businesses and rich individuals that control it. One of the chief worries of policymakers from the mid-1980s onwards was that of capital flight of one kind or another. Banks and their employees might up sticks and move to Geneva; the super-rich could park their money offshore; the bond markets would grow suspicious of public spending plans, and interest rates would rise; celebrities, such as Phil Collins and Tracey Emin, threatened to leave Britain if income tax rose. We are all too conscious of anxieties concerning immigration in British society, yet the latent fear of emigration – by capital and capitalists – has shaped our politics far more decisively over the past thirty or forty years.

Contemporary forms of financial speculation are characterised by an even more radical assertion of exit rights. The mentality of the high-frequency trader or hedge fund manager is wholly focused on leaving on better terms than those on which one arrived, and on minimising the delay or friction in between. To the speculator, falling prices present just as lucrative an opportunity as rising prices, meaning that instability in general is attractive. As long as nothing ever stays the same, you can exit better off than when you entered. The only unprofitable scenario is stasis.

Private investment funds have been a constant feature of Britain's descent into political turmoil, though their precise role remains murky. The American hedge fund billionaire Robert Mercer, a friend of Nigel Farage, was accused of aiding the Leave campaign with data analytics expertise, via the now defunct company Cambridge Analytica. Hedge funds were generous backers of both the Leave and Remain campaigns in 2016, but both sides extracted handsome rewards from the financial turmoil that immediately followed the result. Questions were raised about the relationships between polling companies and hedge funds on the day of the referendum, with fears that pollsters were passing on sensitive information to private clients, to give them first-mover advantage. Bloomberg reported last June that when Farage made his peculiar concession of defeat on the night of the referendum result, he may already have been in possession of polling data from Survation – privately commissioned by multiple clients including hedge funds – which predicted that Leave would win. His announcement briefly buoyed the pound, increasing the profits of any speculators correctly predicting its imminent collapse. The discovery that the fund co-founded by Rees-Mogg, Somerset Capital, was setting up operations in Dublin smacked of 'heads I win, tails you lose' hypocrisy.

Even in the absence of such cynical financial chicanery, there is a certain family resemblance between the logic of the hedge fund and that of hardcore Brexiteers. The hedge fund manager 'shorts' the falling currency or stock, turning failure into money; Brexiteers are constantly distancing themselves from the realities of actually existing Brexit. The two share a mentality that is allergic to commitment, political accountability or – Hirschman's third concept – loyalty. The mindset is infectious, with politicians on every side of the House of Commons currently fixated on short-term moves, seeking to second-guess one another in the hope of benefiting from others' losses. The difference is that in the realm of financial speculation it is possible to take a position on both sides of a dispute – to hedge against the possibility of being wrong – but in the political realm, to claim that one can exit a set of institutions while continuing to benefit from membership of them is having one's cake and eating it. Individuals (including Brexiteers and their wealthy donors) can personally hedge against the consequences of exit, moving their assets overseas, applying for foreign citizenship or even emigrating, but the United Kingdom cannot. At some point, politics comes down to affirmations, not refusals.

The Demise of Liberal Elites

For hundreds of years, modern societies have depended on something that is so ubiquitous, so ordinary, that we scarcely ever stop to notice it: trust. The fact that millions of people are able to believe the same things about reality is a remarkable achievement, but one that is more fragile than is often recognised. At times when public institutions – including the media, government departments and professions – command widespread trust, we rarely question how they achieve this. And yet at the heart of successful liberal democracies lies a remarkable collective leap of faith: that when public officials, reporters, experts and politicians share a piece of information, they are presumed to be doing so in an honest fashion.

The notion that public figures and professionals are basically trustworthy has been integral to the health of representative democracies. After all, the very core of liberal democracy is the idea that a small group of people – politicians – can represent millions of others. If this system is to work, there must be a basic modicum of trust that the small group will act on behalf of the much larger one, at least some of the time. As the past decade has made clear, nothing turns voters against liberalism more rapidly than the appearance of corruption: the suspicion, valid or otherwise, that politicians are exploiting their power for their own private interest.

This isn't just about politics. In fact, much of what we believe to be true about the world is actually taken on trust, via newspapers, experts, officials and broadcasters. While each of us sometimes witnesses events with our own eyes, there are plenty of apparently reasonable truths that we all accept without seeing. In order to believe that the economy has grown by 1 per cent, or to find out about the latest medical advances, we take various things on trust; we don't automatically doubt the moral character of the researchers or reporters involved.

Much of the time, the edifice that we refer to as 'truth' is really an investment of trust. Consider how we come to know the facts about climate change: scientists carefully collect and analyse data, before drafting a paper for anonymous review by other scientists, who assume that the data is authentic. If published, the findings are shared with journalists in press releases, drafted by university press offices. We expect that these findings are then reported honestly and without distortion by broadcasters and newspapers. Civil servants draft ministerial speeches that respond to these facts, including details on what the government has achieved to date.

A modern liberal society is a complex web of trust relations, held together by reports, accounts, records and testimonies. Such systems have always faced political risks and threats. The template of modern expertise can be traced back to the second half of the seventeenth century, when scientists and merchants first established techniques for recording and sharing facts and figures. These were soon adopted by governments, for the purposes of tax collection and rudimentary public finance. But from the start, strict codes of conduct had to be established to ensure that officials and experts were not seeking personal gain or glory (for instance through exaggerating their scientific discoveries), and were bound by strict norms of honesty.

But regardless of how honest parties may be in their dealings with one another, the cultural homogeneity and social intimacy of these gentlemanly networks and clubs has always been grounds for suspicion. Throughout modern history, the bodies tasked with handling public knowledge have always privileged white male graduates, living in global cities and university towns. This does not discredit the knowledge they produce – but where things get trickier is when that homogeneity starts to appear to be a political identity, with a shared set of political goals. This is what is implied by the concept of 'elites': that purportedly separate domains of power – media, business, politics, law, academia – are acting in unison.

A further threat comes from individuals taking advantage of their authority for personal gain. Systems that rely on trust are always open to abuse by those seeking to exploit them. It is a key feature of modern administrations that they use written documents to verify things, but there will always be scope for records to be manipulated, suppressed or fabricated. There is no escaping that possibility altogether. This applies to many fields: at a certain point, the willingness to trust that a newspaper is honestly reporting what a police officer claims to have been told by a credible witness, for example, relies on a leap of faith.

A trend of declining trust has been underway across the Western world for many years, even decades, as copious survey evidence attests. Trust, and its absence, became a preoccupation for policymakers and business leaders during the 1990s and early 2000s. They feared that shrinking trust led to higher rates of crime and less cohesive communities, producing costs that would be picked up by the state. What nobody foresaw was that, when trust sinks beneath a certain point, many people may come to view the entire spectacle of politics and public life as a sham. This happens not because trust in general declines, but because key public figures – notably politicians and journalists – are perceived as untrustworthy. It is those figures specifically tasked with representing society, either as elected representatives or as professional reporters, who have lost credibility.

To understand the crisis liberal democracy faces today – whether we identify this primarily in terms of 'populism' or 'post-truth' – it's not enough simply to bemoan the rising cynicism of the public. We need also to consider some of the reasons *why* trust has been withdrawn. The infrastructure of fact has been undermined in part by a combination of technology and market forces – but we must seriously reckon with the underlying truth of the populists' charge against the establishment today. Too often, the rise of insurgent political parties and demagogues is viewed as the source of liberalism's problems, rather than as a symptom. But by focusing on trust, and the failure of liberal institutions to sustain it, we get a clearer sense of why this is happening now.

The problem today is that, across a number of crucial areas of public life, the basic intuitions of populists have been repeatedly verified. One of the main contributors to this has been the spread of digital technology, creating vast data trails with the latent potential to contradict public statements, and even undermine entire public institutions. Whereas it is impossible to conclusively prove that a politician is morally innocent or that a news report is undistorted, it is far easier to demonstrate the opposite. Scandals, leaks, whistleblowers and revelations of fraud all serve to confirm our worst suspicions. While trust relies on a leap of faith, distrust is supported by ever-mounting piles of evidence. And in Britain, this pile has been expanding much faster than many of us have been prepared to admit.

Confronted by the rise of populist parties and leaders, some commentators have described the crisis facing liberalism in largely economic terms – as a revolt among those 'left behind' by inequality and globalisation. Another camp sees it primarily as the expression of cultural anxieties surrounding identity and immigration. There is some truth in both, of course, but neither gets to the heart of the trust crisis that populists exploit so ruthlessly. A crucial reason liberalism is in danger right now is that the basic honesty of mainstream politicians, journalists and senior officials is no longer taken for granted.

There are copious explanations for Trump, Brexit and so on, but insufficient attention to what populists are actually saying, which focuses relentlessly on the idea of self-serving 'elites' maintaining a status quo that primarily benefits them. On the right, Nigel Farage has accused individual civil servants of seeking to sabotage Brexit for their own private ends. On the left, Jeremy Corbyn repeatedly refers to Britain's 'rigged' economic system. The promise to crack down on corruption and private lobbying is integral to the pitch made by figures such as Donald Trump, Jair Bolsonaro or Viktor Orbán.

One of the great political riddles of recent years is that declining trust in 'elites' is often encouraged and exploited by figures of far more dubious moral character – not to mention far greater wealth – than the technocrats and politicians being ousted. On the face of it, it would seem odd that a sense of 'elite' corruption would play into the hands of hucksters and blaggards such as Donald Trump or Arron Banks. But the authority of these figures owes nothing to their moral character, and everything to their perceived willingness to blow the whistle on corrupt 'insiders' dominating the state and media.

Liberals – including those who occupy 'elite' positions – may comfort themselves with the belief that these charges are ill-founded or exaggerated, or else that the populists offer no solutions to the failures they identify. After all, Trump has not 'drained the swamp' of Washington lobbying. But this is to miss the point of how such rhetoric works, which is to chip away at the core faith on which liberalism depends, namely that power is being used in ways that represent the public interest, and that the facts published by the mainstream media are valid representations of reality.

Populists target various centres of power, including dominant political parties, mainstream media, big business and the institutions of the state, including the judiciary. The chilling phrase 'enemies of the people' has recently been employed by Donald Trump to describe those broadcasters and newspapers he dislikes (such as CNN and the *New York Times*), and by the *Daily Mail* to describe high court judges, following their 2016 ruling that Brexit would require parliamentary consent. But on a deeper level, whether it is the judiciary, the media or the independent civil service that is being attacked is secondary to a more important allegation: that public life in general has become fraudulent.

How does this allegation work? One aspect of it is to dispute the very possibility that a judge, reporter or expert might act in a disinterested, objective fashion. For those whose authority depends on separating their public duties from their personal feelings, having their private views or identities publicised serves as an attack on their credibility. But another aspect is to gradually blur the distinctions between different varieties of expertise and authority, with the implication that politicians, journalists, judges, regulators and officials are effectively all working together.

It is easy for rival professions to argue that they have little in common with each other, and are often antagonistic to each other. Ostensibly, these disparate centres of expertise and power hold each other in check in various ways, producing a pluralist system of checks and balances. Twentieth-century defenders of liberalism, such as the

American political scientist Robert Dahl, often argued that it didn't matter how much power was concentrated in the hands of individual authorities, as long as no single political entity was able to monopolise power. The famous liberal ideal of a 'separation of powers' (distinguishing executive, legislative and judicial branches of government), so influential in the framing of the US constitution, could persist so long as different domains of society hold one another up to critical scrutiny.

But one thing that these diverse professions and authorities do have in common is that they trade primarily in words and symbols. By lumping together journalists, judges, experts and politicians as a single homogeneous 'liberal elite', it is possible to treat them all as indulging in a babble of jargon, political correctness and, ultimately, lies. Their status as public servants is demolished once their claim to speak honestly is thrown into doubt. One way in which this is done is by bringing their private opinions and tastes before the public, something that social media and email render far easier. Tensions and contradictions between the public face of, say, a BBC reporter, and their private opinions and feelings, are much easier to discover in the age of Twitter.

Whether in the media, politics or academia, liberal professions suffer a vulnerability that a figure such as Trump doesn't, in that their authority hangs on their claim to speak the truth. A recent sociological paper by US academics Oliver Hahl, Minjae Kim and Ezra Zuckerman Sivan, draws a distinction between two types of lies.[10] The first, 'special access lies', may be better termed 'insider lies'. This is dishonesty from those trusted to truthfully report facts, who abuse that trust by failing to state what they privately know to be true. (The authors give the example of Bill Clinton's infamous claim that he 'did not have sexual relations with that woman'.)

The second, which they refer to as 'common knowledge lies', are the kinds of lies told by Donald Trump about the size of his election victory or the crowds at his inauguration, or the Vote Leave campaign's false claims about sending '£350m a week to the EU'. These lies do not pretend to be bound by the norm of honesty in the first place, and the listener can make up their own mind what to make of them.

What the paper shows is that, where politics comes to be viewed as the domain of 'insider' liars, there is a seductive authenticity, even a strange kind of honesty, about the 'common knowledge' liar. The rise of highly polished, professional politicians such as Tony Blair and Bill Clinton exacerbated the sense that politics is all about strategic concealment of the truth, something that the Iraq War seemed to confirm as much as anything. Trump or Farage may have a reputation for fabricating things, but they don't (rightly or wrongly) have a reputation for concealing things, which grants them a form of credibility not available to technocrats or professional politicians.

At the same time, and even more corrosively, when elected representatives come to be viewed as 'insider liars', it turns out that other professions whose job it is to report the truth – journalists, experts, officials – also suffer a slump in trust. Indeed, the distinctions between all these fact-peddlers start to look irrelevant in the eyes of those who've given up on the establishment altogether. It is this type of all-encompassing disbelief that creates the opportunity for right-wing populism in particular. Trump voters are more than twice as likely to distrust the media as those who voted for Clinton in 2016, according to the annual Edelman Trust Barometer, which adds that the four countries currently suffering the most 'extreme trust losses' are Italy, Brazil, South Africa and the US.

It's one thing to measure public attitudes, but quite another to understand what shapes them. Alienation and disillusionment develop slowly, and without any single provocation. No doubt economic stagnation and soaring inequality have played a role – but we should not discount the growing significance of scandals that appear to discredit the honesty and objectivity of 'liberal elites'. The misbehaviour of elites did not 'cause' Brexit, but it is striking, in hindsight, how little attention was paid to the accumulation of scandal and its consequences for trust in the establishment.

Britain's decade of scandal
The 2010 edition of the annual British Social Attitudes survey included an ominous finding. Trust in politicians, already low, had suffered a fresh slump, with a majority of people saying politicians never tell the truth. But at the same time, interest in politics had mysteriously risen. To whom would this newly engaged section of the electorate turn if they had lost trust in 'politicians'? One answer was clearly UKIP, who experienced their greatest electoral gains in the years that followed, to the point of winning the most seats in the 2014 elections for the European Parliament. UKIP's

surge, which initially appeared to threaten the Conservative Party, was integral to David Cameron's decision to hold a referendum on EU membership. One of the decisive (and unexpected) factors in the referendum result was the number of voters who went to the polls for the first time, specifically to vote Leave.

What might have prompted the combination of angry disillusionment and intensifying interest that was visible in the 2010 survey? It predated the toughest years of austerity, but there was clearly one event that did more than any other to weaken trust in politicians: the MPs' expenses scandal, which blew up in May 2009 thanks to a drip-feed of revelations published by the *Daily Telegraph*. Following as it did so soon after a disaster of world-historic proportions – the financial crisis – the full significance of the expenses scandal may have been forgotten. But its ramifications were vast. For one thing, it engulfed many of the highest reaches of power in Westminster: the Speaker of the House of Commons, the home secretary, the secretary of state for communities and local government and the chief secretary to the Treasury all resigned. Not only that, but the rot appeared to have infected all parties equally, validating the feeling that politicians had more in common with each other (regardless of party loyalties) than they did with decent, ordinary people.

Many of the issues that 'elites' deal with are complex, concerning law, regulation and economic analysis. We can all see the fallout of the financial crisis, for instance, but the precise causes are disputed and hard to fathom. By contrast, everybody understands expense claims, and everybody knows lying and exaggerating are among the most basic moral failings; even a child understands they are wrong. This may be unfair to the hundreds of honest MPs and to the dozens whose misdemeanours fell into a murky area around the 'spirit' of the rules. But the sense of a mass stitch-up was deeply – and understandably – entrenched.

The other significant thing about the expenses scandal was the way it set a template for a decade of elite scandals – most of which also involved lies, leaks and dishonest denials. One year later, there was another leak from a vast archive of government data: in 2010, WikiLeaks released hundreds of thousands of US military field reports from Iraq and Afghanistan. With the assistance of newspapers including the *New York Times*, *Der Spiegel*, the *Guardian* and *Le Monde*, these 'war logs' disclosed horrifying details about the conduct of US forces and revealed the Pentagon had falsely denied knowledge of various abuses. While some politicians expressed moral revulsion at what had been exposed, the US and British governments blamed WikiLeaks for endangering their troops, and the leaker, Chelsea Manning, was jailed for espionage.

In 2011, the phone-hacking scandal put the press itself under the spotlight. It was revealed that senior figures in News International and the Metropolitan Police had long been aware of the extent of phone-hacking practices – and they had lied about how much they knew. Among those implicated was the prime minister's communications director, former *News of the World* editor Andy Coulson, who was forced to resign his post and later jailed. By the end of 2011, the *News of the World* had been closed down, the

Leveson inquiry was underway, and the entire Murdoch empire was shaking.

The biggest scandal of 2012 was a different beast altogether, involving unknown men manipulating a number that very few people had even heard of. The number in question, the London interbank offered rate, or Libor, is meant to represent the rate at which banks are willing to loan to each other. What was surreal, in an age of complex derivatives and high-frequency trading algorithms, was that this number was calculated on the basis of estimates declared by each bank on a daily basis, and accepted purely on trust. The revelation that a handful of brokers had conspired to alter Libor for private gain (with possible costs to around 250,000 UK mortgage-holders, among others) may have been difficult to fully comprehend, but it gave the not unreasonable impression of an industry enriching itself in a criminal fashion at the public's expense. Bob Diamond, the CEO of Barclays, the bank at the centre of the conspiracy, resigned in July 2012.

Towards the end of that year, the media was caught in another prolonged crisis, this time at the BBC. Horror greeted the broadcast of the ITV documentary *The Other Side of Jimmy Savile* in October 2012. How many people had known about his predatory sexual behaviour, and for how long? Why had the police abandoned earlier investigations? And why had the BBC's *Newsnight* dropped its own film about Savile, due to be broadcast shortly after his death in 2011? The police swiftly established Operation Yewtree to investigate historic sexual abuse allegations, while the BBC established independent commissions into what had gone wrong. But a sense lingered that neither the BBC nor the police had really wanted to know the truth of these matters for the previous forty years.

It wasn't long before it was the turn of the corporate world. In September 2014, a whistleblower revealed that Tesco had exaggerated its half-yearly profits by £250 million, increasing the figure by around a third. An accounting fiddle on this scale clearly had roots at a senior managerial level. Sure enough, four senior executives were suspended the same month and three were charged with fraud two years later. A year later, it emerged that Volkswagen had systematically and deliberately tinkered with emissions controls in their vehicles, so as to dupe regulators in tests, but then pollute liberally the rest of the time. The CEO, Martin Winterkorn, resigned.

'We didn't really learn anything from WikiLeaks we didn't already presume to be true', the philosopher Slavoj Žižek observed in 2014. 'But it is one thing to know it in general and another to get concrete data.'[11] The nature of all these scandals suggests the emergence of a new form of 'facts', in the shape of a leaked archive – one that, crucially, does not depend on trusting the second-hand report of a journalist or official. These revelations are powerful and consequential precisely because they appear to directly confirm our fears and suspicions. Resentment towards 'liberal elites' would no doubt brew even in the absence of supporting evidence. But when that evidence arises, things become far angrier, even when the data – as in the case of Hillary Clinton's emails – isn't actually very shocking.

This is by no means an exhaustive list of the scandals

of the past decade, nor are they all of equal significance. But viewing them together provides a better sense of how the suspicions of populists cut through. Whether or not we continue to trust in politicians, journalists or officials, we have grown increasingly used to this pattern in which a curtain is dramatically pulled back, to reveal those who have been lying to or defrauding the public. Another pattern also begins to emerge. It's not just that isolated individuals are unmasked as corrupt or self-interested (something that is as old as politics), but that the establishment itself starts to appear deceitful and dubious. The distinctive scandals of the twenty-first century are a combination of some very basic and timeless moral failings (greed and dishonesty) with technologies of exposure that expose malpractice on an unprecedented scale, and with far more dramatic results.

Perhaps the most important feature of all these revelations was that they were definitely scandals, and not merely failures: they involved deliberate efforts to defraud or mislead. Several involved sustained cover-ups, delaying the moment of truth for as long as possible. Several ended with high-profile figures behind bars. Jail terms satisfy some of the public demand that the 'elites' pay for their dishonesty, but they don't repair the trust that has been damaged. On the contrary, there's a risk that they affirm the cry for retribution, after which the quest for punishment is only ramped up further. Chants of 'lock her up' reverberated around Trump rallies, long after the 2016 election was over.

In addition to their conscious and deliberate nature, a second striking feature of these scandals was the ambiguous role played by the media. On the one hand, the reputation of the media has taken a pummelling over the past decade, egged on by populists and conspiracy theorists who accuse the 'mainstream media' of being allied to professional political leaders, and who now have the benefit of social media through which to spread this message. The moral authority of newspapers may never have been high, but the grisly revelations that journalists hacked the phone of murdered schoolgirl Milly Dowler represented a new low in the public standing of the press. The Leveson inquiry, followed soon after by the Savile revelations and Operation Yewtree, generated a sense of a media class who were adept at exposing others, but equally expert at concealing the truth of their own behaviours.

On the other hand, it was newspapers and broadcasters that enabled all of this to come to light at all. The extent of phone hacking was eventually exposed by the *Guardian*, the MPs' expenses by the *Telegraph*, Jimmy Savile by ITV, and the 'war logs' reported with the aid of several newspapers around the world simultaneously. But the media was playing a different kind of role from the one traditionally played by journalists and newspapers, with very different implications for the status of truth in society. A backlog of data and allegations had built up in secret, until eventually a whistle was blown. An archive existed that the authorities refused to acknowledge, until they couldn't resist the pressure to do so any longer. Journalists and whistleblowers were instrumental in removing the pressure valve, but from that point on, truth poured out unpredictably. While such torrents are underway, there is no way of knowing how far they may spread or how long they may last.

The era of 'big data' is also the era of 'leaks'. Where traditional 'sleaze' could topple a minister, several of the defining scandals of the past decade have been on a scale so vast that they exceed any individual's responsibility. The Edward Snowden revelations of 2013, the Panama Papers leak of 2015 and the HSBC files (revealing organised tax evasion) all involved the release of tens of thousands or even millions of documents. Paper-based bureaucracies never faced threats to their legitimacy on this scale.

The power of commissions and inquiries to make sense of so much data is not to be understated, nor is the integrity of those newspapers and whistleblowers that helped bring misdemeanours to light. In cases such as MPs' expenses, some newspapers even invited their readers to help search these vast archives for treasure troves, like human algorithms sorting through data. But it is hard to imagine that the net effect of so many revelations was to build trust in any publicly visible institutions. On the contrary, the discovery that 'elites' have been blocking access to a mine of incriminating data is perfect fodder for conspiracy theories. In his 2010 memoir, *A Journey*, Tony Blair confessed that legislating for freedom of information was one of his biggest regrets, which gave a glimpse of how transparency is viewed from the centre of power.

Following the release of the war logs by WikiLeaks, nobody in any position of power claimed that the data wasn't accurate (it was, after all, the data, and not a journalistic report). Nor did they offer any moral justification for what was revealed. Defence departments were left making the flimsiest of arguments – that it was better for everyone if they didn't know how war was conducted. It may well be that the House of Commons was not fairly represented by the MPs' expenses scandal, that most City brokers are honest, or that the VW emissions scam was a one-off within the car industry. But scandals don't work through producing fair or representative pictures of the world; they do so by blowing the lid on hidden truths and lies. Where whistleblowing and leaking become the dominant form of truth-telling, the authority of professional truth-tellers – reporters, experts, professionals, broadcasters – is thrown into question.

Post-liberal elites

The term 'illiberal democracy' is now frequently invoked to describe states such as Hungary under Viktor Orbán or Turkey under Recep Tayyip Erdoğan. In contrast to liberal democracy, this model of authoritarian populism targets the independence of the judiciary and the media, ostensibly on behalf of 'the people'. Brexit has been caused partly by distrust in 'liberal elites', but the anxiety is that it is also accelerating a drift towards 'illiberalism'. There is a feeling at large, albeit among outspoken Remainers, that the BBC has treated the Leave campaign and Brexit itself with kid gloves, for fear of provoking animosity. More worrying was the discovery by openDemocracy in October that the Metropolitan Police were delaying their investigation into alleged breaches of electoral law by the Leave campaign due to what a Met spokesperson called 'political sensitivities'.[12] The risk at the present juncture is that key civic institutions will seek to avoid exercising scrutiny and due process, for fear of upsetting their opponents.

Britain is not an 'illiberal democracy', but the credibility of our elites is still in trouble, and efforts to placate their populist opponents may only make matters worse. At the more extreme end of the spectrum, the far-right activist Stephen Yaxley-Lennon, also known as Tommy Robinson, has used his celebrity and social media reach to cast doubt on the judiciary and the BBC at once. Yaxley-Lennon has positioned himself as a freedom fighter, revealing 'the truth' about Muslim men accused of grooming underage girls, by violating legal rules that restrict reporting details of ongoing trials. Yaxley-Lennon was found guilty of contempt of court and jailed (he was later released after the Court of Appeal ordered a retrial, and the case has been referred to the attorney general), but this only deepened his appeal for those who believed the establishment was complicit in a cover-up, and ordinary people were being deliberately duped.

The political concern right now is that suspicions of this nature – that the truth is being deliberately hidden by an alliance of 'elites' – are no longer the preserve of conspiracy theorists, but becoming increasingly common. Our current crisis has too many causes to enumerate here, and it is impossible to apportion blame for a collective collapse of trust – which is as much a symptom of changes in media technologies as it is of any moral failings on the part of elites. But what is emerging now is what Michel Foucault would have called a new 'regime of truth' – a different way of organising knowledge and trust in society. The advent of experts and government administrators in the seventeenth century created the platform for a distinctive liberal solution to this problem, which rested on the assumption that knowledge would reside in public records, newspapers, government files and journals. But once the integrity of these people and these instruments is cast into doubt, an opportunity arises for a new class of political figures and technologies to demand trust instead.

The project that was launched over three centuries ago, of trusting elite individuals to know, report and judge things on our behalf, may not be viable in the long term, at least not in its existing form. It is tempting to indulge the fantasy that we can reverse the forces that have undermined it, or else batter them into retreat with an even bigger arsenal of facts. But this is to ignore the more fundamental ways in which the nature of trust is changing.

The main feature of the emerging regime is that truth is now assumed to reside in hidden archives of data, rather than in publicly available facts. This is what is affirmed by scandals such as MPs' expenses and the leak of the Iraq War logs – and more recently in the #MeToo movement, which also occurred through a sudden and voluminous series of revelations, generating a crisis of trust. The truth was out there, just not in the public domain. In the age of email, social media and camera phones, it is now common sense to assume that virtually all social activity is generating raw data, which exists out there somewhere. Truth becomes like the lava below the earth's crust, which periodically bursts through as a volcano.

What role does this leave for the traditional, analogue purveyors of facts and figures? What does it mean to 'report' the news in an age of reflexive disbelief? Newspapers have been grappling with this question for some time now; some have decided to refashion themselves as portals to the raw data, or curators of other people's content. But it is no longer intuitively obvious to the public why they should be prepared to take a journalist's word for something, when they can witness the thing itself in digital form. There may be good answers to these questions, but they are not obvious ones.

Instead, a new type of heroic truth-teller has emerged in tandem with these trends. This is the individual who appears brave enough to call bullshit on the rest of the establishment – whether that be government agencies, newspapers, business, political parties or anything else. Some are whistleblowers, others are political leaders, and others are more like conspiracy theorists or trolls. The problem is that everyone has a different heroic truth-teller, because we're all preoccupied by different bullshit. There is no political alignment between figures such as Chelsea Manning and Nigel Farage; what they share is only a willingness to defy the establishment and break consensus.

If a world where everyone has their own truth-tellers sounds dangerously like relativism, that's because it is. But the roots of this new and often unsettling 'regime of truth' don't only lie with the rise of populism or the age of big data. Elites have largely failed to understand that this crisis is about trust rather than facts – which may be why they did not detect the rapid erosion of their own credibility.

Unless liberal institutions and their defenders are willing to reckon with their own inability to sustain trust, the events of the past decade will remain opaque to them. And unless those institutions can rediscover aspects of the original liberal impulse – to keep different domains of power separate, and put the disinterested pursuit of knowledge before the pursuit of profit – then the present trends will only intensify, and no quantity of facts will be sufficient to resist. Power and authority will accrue to a combination of decreasingly liberal states and digital platforms – interrupted only by the occasional outcry as whistles are blown and outrages exposed.

Comedy or Demagoguery?

Back in the early 1990s, when Rob Newman and David Baddiel were selling out vast arenas, it was briefly posited that 'comedy is the new rock 'n' roll'. Today one might surmise that 'politics is the new comedy'. In addition to the reality television star in the White House, the party with the largest vote share in Italy's 2018 elections – Five Star – was founded by a former comedian, and the president of Ukraine is a former comedian. The funny side of Boris Johnson has been fading for some time. But it is still clear that the man currently favourite to be Britain's next prime minister has milked his comedy value effectively over the past twenty years, with *Have I Got News for You* playing a particularly important role in raising the national profile of the blustering blond buffoon.

There is nothing funny about the political consequences of men such as Donald Trump and Johnson, but it is hard to deny that they generate plenty of the kind of 'content' that entertains their opponents on the liberal left. Shows such as *Have I Got News For You*, or *The Daily Show* in the United

States, have no doubt provided a crucial pressure valve for those on the liberal left seeking to cope with political events that seem beyond reason. But they also risk creating an unspoken partnership between reckless conservative politicians and their critics, with the latter using mockery and laughter to distance themselves from the seriousness of the situation, while raising the profile of such politicians further.

Twitter is an especially fraught medium in this regard, where the dominant mood is a mixture of irony and outrage that finds frequent expression in humorous ridicule of opposing political arguments. Even before the trolls and meme-makers have got to work, one sure-fire way to go viral around social media is to make a public blunder of some kind. Who's to say that these are necessarily 'mistakes'? The clown has an immediate advantage in the attention economy. As Richard Seymour has argued, 'Through our incensed critique, we enter into a new kind of *affective symbiosis* with the shit-stirrers.'[13]

Politics and comedy are dissolving into one another in disturbing ways. But perhaps we can go even further: in key respects, the public sphere has been reconfigured over the past twenty years around the template of the stand-up comedy club. The precedent for our turbulent, unruly, hilarious, dangerous political moment lies in those late-night sessions, above pubs and underground, where an individual seeks to tame and tickle a crowd, occasionally getting diverted into dealing with a heckler. The root cause of this fusion of comedy with politics is the digitisation of our public sphere, with all the innovations and expansions that have gone with it.

In its idealised liberal form, the 'public sphere' granted an unrivalled power to the technology of the printing press and the judgement of the critic. Books, magazines, journals and newspapers were the original conduits of national and international public argument, with respect to knowledge, culture and politics. Print publications allowed scholars to criticise and learn from one another. They allowed artistic pioneers to acquire reputation. Despite the model of the European salon or coffee shop celebrated by Jürgen Habermas and Richard Sennett, it was print technology that allowed arguments to be conducted over time and space.

The possibility of a reasoned, thoughtful critique of a novel, political speech, artwork or policy depended originally on the specific affordances of the press. Daily newspapers allowed vast publics to inhabit a shared chronology (facilitating the 'imagined community' that Benedict Anderson saw as the central artefact of nations), but one which operated according to a particular metronomic punctuality.[14] Debates could continue via the letters pages of newspapers or – more slowly – the pages of scholarly journals for months or years. The recent valorisation of live debate, in the hands of celebrities such as Richard Dawkins and Jordan Peterson, is more a symptom of a given business model, where audiences (and potential book buyers) are attracted to the frisson of staged intellectual combat, than it is a testimony to 'reason' or 'enlightenment'.

Critique necessarily involves delay. Even where an artwork involves performance, such as a concert or piece of theatre, and where its effect is visceral and dramatic, a critic still requires some time to convert their experience into thoughts, reflections and judgement. It's perfectly possible for a critic to be greatly affected by something in the moment – for instance a political speech or film – while concluding, on reflection, that it was bad. Politicians who deploy emotional techniques too readily are accused of demagoguery, while art that panders to nostalgia or romantic cliché is accused of being schmaltzy or sentimental.

In this analogue context, stand-up comedy was always a bit of an anomaly. What, after all, is the point of *critique* when it comes to live comedy? If an audience is doubled up in laughter, in what sense could the critic declare the comedy unworthy? If a comedian is dying on their feet, how could they possibly be judged to be any good? Unlike virtually any other cultural form, stand-up comedy is real-time, or it is nothing at all. Stand-up comedy comes with its own inbuilt form of critical feedback, namely laughter.

Except laughter is not really critical feedback at all. For one thing, it operates via the body as much as the mind, gripping our chests, evading conscious control. For another, it emanates from the crowd as much as from the individual, with all of the unpredictable patterns that go with crowd behaviour. But what most distinguishes laughter from a judgement is that judgements can be 'positive' or 'negative', pinpointing merits and weaknesses. A book review can lavish praise or deliver a hatchet-job. A comedy audience, on the other hand, can either laugh … or not. The quality of a stand-up comedian is reflected in *how much positive feedback they get*. A bad comedian doesn't receive bad feedback; they receive no feedback.

There is, of course, an exception to this which arises when

hecklers intervene. And yet the heckle is not a criticism, so much as an attention-grabbing disruption. It throws down a challenge to the comedian to react and seize control of the situation. If they succeed in doing so, they can appear brave and smart in their ability to think quickly. The unrehearsed nature of the heckle and put-down grants them an air of authenticity and excitement, that the scripted performance cannot attain on its own. The triumphant comedian takes on heroic qualities in the eyes of their audience, being not just brave enough to do stand-up at all, but seemingly possessed of a real-time wit that is displayed like a master swordsman. There is a suspension of disbelief at work, where the audience members convince themselves that the hero is *really like this*, that they are not witnessing the carefully honed fruits of thousands of gigs (it is a motto within Britain's stand-up community that you don't really know what you're doing on stage until you've done 500 gigs), but a genuinely brilliant person seizing control of a crowd. The persona and the person are one and the same.

There is, nevertheless, one set of observers whose critical judgement is hugely valued by stand-up comedians, namely other stand-up comedians. While the newspaper critic can be dismissed as a loser and a curmudgeon, who lacks the guts to ever stand on a stage and refuses to acknowledge the ultimate importance of audience reaction, the rival stand-up understands the craft and courage of doing comedy. Comedians seek the approval of other comedians more than anyone else, for only their peers (and especially their more established peers) truly grasp the artistry of the stand-up performance. An audience can provide a constant flow of affirmative laughter, but only the rival can offer that most valued commodity: recognition.

This template for public performance, reaction, disruption and recognition is now being recreated in various situations, not least in and around the institutions of democracy. This might go some way to explaining why professional and quasi-comedians now seem to possess some kind of advantage in the new political landscape.

First of all, the explosion of media bandwidth over the past twenty years, which has normalised the twenty-four-hour news cycle, has meant that the public sphere is less dominated by critics than by real-time reaction. Evidently, some people have more influence over the reaction than others: just as there are professional 'influencers', there are now professional 'reactors' such as Piers Morgan and Toby Young, whose main role in public life is to divert attention in certain directions, and encourage audience response. Twitter provides a constant, rolling, twenty-four-seven version of the comedy club audience, laughing back at the figures on the stage, periodically hurling chunks of abuse from the anonymity of the unlit auditorium. None of this is criticism as such, and most of it would be meaningless if it was delayed, even by just a few hours. Like laughter, it is real-time feedback, that all counts as attention of one kind or another.

Technologies are developing all the time to facilitate greater ease of feedback, along with the capacity to quantify and analyse it. The Facebook 'reaction' buttons (like, angry, wow, laughter, sad) are one example, while Twitter 'likes' and 'retweets' are another. Facial analytics and other behavioural monitoring tools expand the capacity to harvest real-time sentiment from audiences. As far as the digital platforms are concerned, the objective here is really no different from that of a comedy club manager: to ensure that as many people are bringing their reactions to *this* location, and not to a rival one. What a 'like' or 'favourite' *means*, or *why* it was given, is beside the point. Like the laughter that ripples through a comedy club, it was how things felt at the time.

Like the audience in the club, the online crowd is amenable to waves of feeling, which seize its members in ways that they don't expect and can't always easily explain. As Seymour argues, this can only really be understood as a 'somatic' phenomenon, that is, a process that passes from one physical body to another, only now mediated by touchscreens, wireless networks and algorithms, creating long-distance, real-time crowds. Unlike publishers, the platforms are not looking for positive judgement of the content they host, but intensity of sentiment, regardless of whether it is 'positive' or 'negative' (Facebook, presumably, sees 'angry' or 'sad' reactions as of equal value to 'like'). With YouTube, Facebook and Twitter coming under increasing fire for their hosting of hateful and violent content, it needs to be remembered that – as for the comedy club – the only bad content, from the perspective of their business model, is that which provokes no engagement or feedback at all.

One of the challenges presented to politicians by the twenty-four-hour, real-time public sphere is that they can be 'heckled' at any time. They're never entirely off-stage. The phenomenon of MPs being harassed in the street is an ugly and troubling political development, but it is partly an effect of ubiquitous smartphones and YouTube. Invariably, the harasser (or their accomplice) is filming the event, in the hope of gaining some online respect. Court hearings now face similar threats from political movements, such as Stephen Yaxley-Lennon's ('Tommy Robinson'), aimed at politicising them. The same is true of most disruptions of campus events.

Politicians who can navigate real-time disturbances, on camera, while maintaining their composure can reap huge political dividends. Never has Jeremy Corbyn outshone Theresa May as much as he did in the summer of 2017, following footage of the two leaders visiting Grenfell Tower survivors. Corbyn appeared relaxed and physically intimate with people, while May looked uncomfortable and formal. Like the stand-up going off script, the heroism of leaders in this climate is demonstrated when protocol is abandoned, and everything comes down to live performance. It is a sign of how badly May is suited to the present media climate that she allegedly speaks from a script even during private meetings.

Trump's 2016 rallies took the cult of live performance to ridiculous lengths. Frequently compared to the atmosphere at WWE wrestling bouts, these events were a manic combination of the scripted, the unscripted and the scripted 'unscripted', complete with hecklers being dragged out by security, and Trump taking every opportunity to be as Trump as possible. As with live comedy, so for wrestling and Trump rallies: the critic is blindsided by an event where everything is in the delivery, and the lasting contribution is neither here nor there.

It's not news that 'authenticity' is a highly prized attribute in this era of anti-politics. But as with the authenticity of the stand-up comedian, this is a complicated asset that usually takes considerable practice to develop. Just as the greatest achievement of a stand-up is to convince the audience that the whole thing is spontaneous – that they're *really* getting to hang out with a brilliant wit – a figure such as Boris Johnson has had plenty of opportunity to tinker with the character known as 'Boris'. As any stand-up will tell you, the trick is to find the part or version of yourself that you're most confident and comfortable sharing, which can take time to identify. It's neither 'fake' nor 'real', but something else altogether.

And as with stand-up comedy, the figure that the demagogic leader most reveres – and whose approval he most seeks – is the other demagogic leader. Trump, Vladimir Putin, Viktor Orbán, Jair Bolsonaro and, in a milder sense, Johnson, are each examples of a type of populist 'strong man', who holds the liberal media in disdain and seeks to position himself above oppositional parliamentary politics. But each of them has a weakness when it comes to the others, revelling in the mutual flattery that can only be offered by a national leader of a similar psychology.

The danger this whole situation poses is that we constantly encounter serious issues packaged up with unserious ones. The mood of Brexit is one of gloomy hilarity, generating a media cycle of absurdity, outrage, ridicule and fear, but which never quite seems to descend on anything real or permanent. One reason for this affective state is that, where Brexit is concerned, there really isn't much time, making critical distance and delay harder to come by. It is a situation ripe for demagoguery, where a skilled and 'authentic' personality can face down opponents live, on camera. A further risk is that harmful policies only become publicly denounced once they've become outrageous, and even then the denunciators are often vying for attention.

It's been reported that 54 per cent of British voters believe that the UK now needs a 'strong leader willing to break the rules'.[15] What might such a figure look like? Images of 'strong men' rulers are usually of military types, with scant regard for the rule of law. But it's just as likely (perhaps more so) that such a figure could arise in Britain in the guise of a heroic wit, who successfully puts dissenting 'hecklers' in their place with great panache. Those who have honed such personas over years will be well placed to seize this political moment. Avoiding this will require the rest of us, where possible, to resist getting seduced by humour, rhetorical reflexes and bravado. We need to find an alternative to the kind of 'heckling' reaction that dominates the twenty-four-seven news cycle, especially on social media, which the performer ultimately benefits from. In place of staged combat, we need to find the time and the space to carry out critical analysis. A bit of humourlessness might go a long way.

3

'The People' versus 'Politics'

Had Britain departed the EU on 31 March 2019, as Theresa May had hoped, it wouldn't have held European elections the following May. The results of those elections prompted many observers to question whether two-party politics (and the Conservative Party in particular) were finished. Nigel Farage's new Brexit Party came top with 32 per cent of the vote, and the Conservatives fifth with just 9 per cent; May resigned the following day. Spring 2019 confirmed something that was lurking within Brexit all along: that it was never simply a policy choice or regulatory problem to solve, but an attack on the entire liberal apparatus of government, professional party politics and mainstream media. It wasn't clear how any politician could satisfy a desire to explode politics. The answer concocted by Boris Johnson and Dominic Cummings over the summer of 2019 was to craft a whole new style of leadership – against the liberal media, against Parliament and even against the law. The comical, destructive, mendacious Facebook star known as 'Boris' was pitted against the establishment. By the time of the

*December 2019 election, the Johnson campaign was operat-
ing less as a normal political party, and more as a single-issue
guerrilla marketing outfit.*

Democracy without Representation

It is a necessary principle of representative democracy that
small minorities – parties, politicians, parliaments – stand
for the whole. The system works best when there is an
element of illusion involved, such that the narrow range
of characters and ideas on the public stage is viewed as
a decent proxy for society at large. Too much scrutiny –
when a dodgy expense claim comes to light, say, or an email
indiscretion – and the illusion is liable to be dispelled.

But when the stage is set correctly, the illusion can be
very powerful. Margaret Thatcher and Tony Blair oversaw
devastating electoral machines, which delivered four huge
parliamentary majorities in the space of twenty years. Both
appeared to establish a new consensus as to what constituted
good leadership and policy. The fact that neither leader ever
won the votes of more than 31 per cent of the electorate was
obscured, not only by Britain's archaic voting system, but
by a set of media institutions for which 'national politics'
meant Westminster. What is taken to have been an epoch-
defining national 'ism' can, on closer inspection, appear
more like a canny handling of newspaper owners and party
donors. But that's the way the illusion works. It generates
the mass psychological impression that we have all given
our consent. Another term for this is 'hegemony'.

The tradition of Marxist state theory has grappled with a

related question: how do policies that serve a narrow set of economic interests come to be regarded as common sense, as if they benefited the economy as a whole? It's not just that capitalist states defend the interests of capital, but that they tend to favour one type of capital at the expense of others. Until recently, the consensus on 'good' economic policy concealed a mentality that always in effect privileged finance. One economic part was treated as a proxy for the economic whole. If it is to retain credibility, this equivalence requires careful political and cultural management.

British democracy is currently disillusioned. The parties that dominated the past century of national politics are in crisis; an astonishing YouGov poll conducted in May 2019 put both Labour and the Conservatives on 19 per cent, behind the Liberal Democrats and Nigel Farage's Brexit Party. An Opinium poll later put the Brexit Party out in front on 26 per cent. Farage's outfit has adopted the model of a platform start-up, as pioneered by the Italian Five Star Movement, to disrupt electoral politics at unprecedented speed. Theresa May and Jeremy Corbyn now hold the record for the most unpopular leadership duo ever, breaking the record set by Thatcher and Michael Foot in December 1981.

The roots of this disillusionment extend back many years, well before the 2016 referendum. Nevertheless, a plebiscite does particular violence to the faith on which parliamentary democracy depends. It takes the complex patchwork of parties, constituencies and coalitions of interest, and in an instant subordinates the lot to a single popular demand. It's doubtful that David Cameron ever thought this far ahead, but in his passion for referendums (four were held during his premiership) he was testing parliamentary sovereignty to breaking point. Under these circumstances, political hegemony is impossible. No leader, party or ideology can credibly be presented as serving the common good. There are only factions battling other factions. Meanwhile, the priorities of the national newspapers and broadcasters seem increasingly out of sync with those of the electorate, who can now turn to a plethora of online sources. Business lobbies have rarely been so powerless over the fundamentals of economic policy.

In principle, this sudden awakening of pluralism could be good news, a 'British Spring' that breaks through the screen onto which 'politics' has long been projected by political and media machines, to reveal how power actually works. That's a hope worth hanging on to. The danger is that while faith in the overall system may have evaporated, its rusty constitutional mechanics are still in place.

Britain's next prime minister will be elected by the 160,000 members of the Conservative Party. According to YouGov, 59 per cent of these members voted for the Brexit Party in the April 2019 European elections. The Tories have made numerous bad leadership appointments in the last twenty years (think of Iain Duncan Smith), but have corrected them once the pragmatic question of electoral success entered the equation. That pressure pushes the party towards the swing voter of the centre ground, the 'Mondeo Man' or 'Worcester Woman' fetishised by party pollsters in the 1990s and early 2000s. Is any of this still relevant? How much do Tory members even care about general elections, compared to their passion for a no-deal Brexit? There are plenty of reasons not to elect Boris Johnson as prime minister, but much of the Conservative electorate is focused only on his one perceived virtue: his celebration of no deal.

The Conservative leadership contest is already turning into a competition on who can make the most autocratic statement on Brexit. Esther McVey has said that, as prime minister, she would sack every Remainer from the cabinet. Candidates idly toss around the prospect of proroguing Parliament, so as to ensure Britain's timely exit. This prospect is coming to perform the moral function that torture plays in American Republican primary debates: it's something candidates are obliged to clarify their position on, being wary of looking soft. It was no surprise that, in the recent leadership hustings, both Dominic Raab and Andrea Leadsom took the bait, declaring themselves in favour of Parliament being suspended by the Queen. As an indication of what's happening to the Tory party, the more disturbing sight was of Jeremy Hunt – ostensibly a pragmatist – refusing to rule it out. And so the party's long descent into ideological madness reaches a new nadir, where a sitting foreign secretary toys with declaring a state of exception, purely to exorcise some imagined European demon.

Take Nigel Farage. His achievement in winning the European elections with a four-month-old party is remarkable. But in comparison with the hapless Change UK, established a month later and now surely about to fold, his job was straightforward. The Brexit Party's branding and social media tactics were state of the art, but the messaging wrote itself: when Britain failed to leave the EU on 29 March it was because Westminster politicians had betrayed the 52 per cent who had voted Leave. What's more, where speedy selection of nationwide candidates is a task fraught with risk for a liberal start-up such as Change UK (two of its candidates had to be replaced after 'inappropriate' and 'offensive' tweets came to light), the Brexit Party draws energy and gains attention from its collection of cranks and firebrands.

The Brexit Party is a mixture of business start-up and social movement; it serves as a pressure valve, releasing pent-up frustration with traditional politics into the electoral system. Farage is in full control of the valve. He now possesses exceptional autonomy, quite free of the constraints that the media, party machines and constitutions have imposed on ambitious leaders in the past. Rival parties can neither ignore nor negotiate with this new presence. It makes the political weather.

No deal will always be a niche minority position, within the electorate and even more so in Parliament. And yet this is currently where all the momentum in British politics lies. This is a freakish and frightening situation. It isn't just that no deal is unrepresentative of mainstream public opinion (by which one might mean the preferences of the risk-averse swing voter of yesterday), but that the forces behind it make no real claim to be representative either. No dealers are the most disillusioned of all: many believe they have seen through the con of parliamentary democracy and perceive themselves as freedom fighters against a mendacious and oppressive majority. This is an anti-hegemonic project. Little wonder that the Brexit Party fielded two former members of the Revolutionary Communist Party – Claire Fox and James Heartfield – among its MEP candidates. Support for no deal correlates directly with age, to the point where the majority of over-sixties now express support for Farage. It is also most entrenched among the financially secure. The typical no dealer is a hybrid of Che Guevara and a *Telegraph*-reading retiree from Sevenoaks.

Where does this momentum come from? The bitter irony is that it is partly the consequence of the legalistic nature of the EU itself. In such a dysfunctional political situation as the UK's, no deal has the immense advantage of being the default outcome if nothing else can be agreed on. The most authoritarian force in British politics just now is Article 50 itself, with its two-year (since extended by seven months) window of opportunity to draft and ratify a withdrawal agreement. As it turns out, two years is more than enough time to initiate a national existential crisis, but not nearly enough time to sort one out. The flowering of any 'British Spring' will be cruelly curtailed before very long.

For both Thatcher and Blair, converting 30 per cent of the nation's support into a transformative governing paradigm took considerable time, effort and political nous. In order to create a new common sense, 'Thatcherism' or 'Blairism' had to build up delicate alliances with key business interests, dominant media players, intellectuals and centres of expertise, all the while keeping in mind the median voter, with his or her everyday middle-class concerns about economic security. By contrast, come November this year, Farage, Johnson and their allies may well have achieved a far greater disruption of the political and economic status quo than Thatcher or Blair ever managed, with a smaller popular mandate and far less effort. They don't need think-tanks, policy breakfasts, the CBI or party discipline. They don't even need ideas. All they have to do, in pursuit of their goal, is to carry on being themselves, undermining trust, contaminating the grounds of agreement.

Given that any 'soft Brexit' is now seen as 'betrayal' by the Brexit Party and its sympathisers in the Conservative Party, it's impossible to imagine any consensual compromise. Say what you like about Theresa May's deal, but it was at least a viable route out of the European Union – just not an authentic one, as far as Farage et al. are concerned. No one appears to relish the prospect of a second referendum, though Farage would certainly build yet more political capital out of it if there were one. But what's the alternative? While it might sound implausible, given the current depth of anti-government feeling, the most reasonable solution would be to revoke Article 50 and call a general election, with the parties – four or five mid-sized ones, as things stand – all laying out their visions for Britain's relationship with Europe in their manifestos.

The question for the longer term is the one that has been repeatedly asked since Corbyn's election as Labour leader in 2015: is this type of politics a blip, or is this the new normal? Can we become re-illusioned with representative democracy? Or is all politics now a form of anti-politics? The circumstances of Brexit are unique, as is the sense of emergency cultivated by the time limit imposed by Article 50. It is possible that the most recent elections and polls exaggerate the influence that Brexit will play over future voting behaviour. But there are good reasons to believe that we are witnessing a new type of democracy.

Chief among these reasons is the rise of what the sociologist Paolo Gerbaudo has called the 'digital party' or 'platform party', of which Farage's Brexit Party is arguably the most impressive example to date.[1] According to Gerbaudo, such a party 'is to the current informational era of ubiquitous networks, social media and smartphone apps what the mass party was to the industrial era or the cynically professionalised "television party" was during the post–Cold War era of high neoliberalism'.[2] It is like a tech start-up, aimed at rapid growth, with email sign-ups and PayPal donations replacing formal membership. And, in accordance with the creed of Silicon Valley, its purpose is to disrupt.

Digital logic is also transforming the broader public sphere in which parties operate. Print and broadcast media have always depended on editorial judgement regarding what 'the public' is or should be interested in. To prosper in such a media system, politicians need to be ordinary and inoffensive to the mainstream. The 'cynically professionalised' politics to which Gerbaudo refers include carefully staged displays of normality by figures such as Blair and Bill Clinton. The bland sight of the 2010 Cameron-Clegg identikit double act was perhaps the UK's final sighting of this type of leadership.

By contrast, in an age of limitless bandwidth and ubiquitous data capture, the challenge for politicians (or anyone else) is to get noticed and exert influence. This calls for a very different set of political and personal talents: confrontation, wit, defiance, spontaneity and rule-breaking. The politician who wants to target the swing voter via television tries to seem as normal as possible. The politician who seeks to mobilise support online will do precisely the opposite. While it's true that Farage has made mileage out of his 'ordinary' cultural habits ('a fag and a pint'), a Trumpian refusal to play by the rules is his more potent quality.

The internet is an anti-hegemonic technology. It grants far more power to the consensus-breaker than to the consensus-maker. As the data analytics industry understands, it is a brilliant machine for mapping unusual clusters of feeling and behaviour, but far less suited to establishing averages and generalities. The internet fragments the 'middle ground' as a space of political argument, and grants a disproportionately loud voice to the niche and the crank. There are illusions galore here, but no sanctuary for the crucial synecdochical one on which representative democracy depends. Notions of 'common sense' and 'the average voter' lose their sway.

These trends may be good for the vitality of democracy in various ways, but not necessarily for parliamentary democracy, and less still for effective government in the traditional sense. It could be that the UK faces a long future of minority governments and coalitions, in which every party is defined as a vessel for the particular discontents of its supporters. This would be bad news for Britain's 'natural party of government', the Conservatives. It also poses a new challenge for capital, which has to try to present its interests as coinciding with those of the public. No doubt a solid majority of people out there are supportive of the basic foundations of parliamentary democracy, fervently opposed to no deal and appalled by the demagogic posturing of Johnson and

Farage. The question is whether they can find a vehicle to represent their position, and find it fast.

The Conservative Selectorate

It seems there is only one voter who matters in British politics right now: a Brexit-obsessed, fifty-something white man living in rural southern England. Why? Because a quirk of Britain's unwritten constitution is that prime ministers are often appointed by their parties without facing general election. John Major, Gordon Brown and Theresa May were all selected by their party to take charge as a result of their predecessor resigning. Only Major was ever able to achieve any clear electoral success of his own.

May's resignation in May meant that, once again, a new prime minister will soon be appointed without a democratic mandate. The overwhelming favourite is Boris Johnson, the controversial journalist-turned-politician, with a life-long weakness for causing offence and then laughing off the consequences. Unless there is a great upset, Johnson's appointment will be announced on 23 July, leaving this notoriously reckless figure to navigate Britain's exit from the European Union, which he has committed to delivering by the 31 October deadline.

Each political party has its own way of handling the process. Brown insisted that he be handed the job by Tony Blair uncontested, which is what happened in 2007. (This was described as a 'gigantic fraud' at the time by none other than Johnson.) For the Conservatives, there is a complicated series of votes among the party's members of Parliament to whittle things down to two candidates, who are then presented to the party's members. The choice before the Conservative membership is between Johnson and Jeremy Hunt, a more trusted but unexciting man, with far less appeal to the Conservative base.

At a time of deep political and economic anxiety, the contest is producing the surreal experience of something that *feels* like democracy – an election campaign season, complete with televised debates and policy announcements – but without any public franchise. In this case, the 'electorate' consists of a mere 160,000 people, just 0.3 per cent of the national electorate, who are significantly older and richer than average.[3] And while Johnson is hounded by questions surrounding his honesty and indiscretions, the Conservative Party membership seems to view his personality as an asset.

This is uncharted territory. Conservative Party rules have changed since Major entered office in 1990, to allow the members to have the final say. (May's rivals all withdrew in 2016, so the members weren't consulted.) At first glance, a leader elected by 160,000 people might seem to have a greater democratic mandate than one appointed by their own colleagues. But as more becomes known about the unusual identities and priorities of the party members, the worry is that Britain is now in the grip of something combining the worst aspects of both oligarchy and representative democracy. It might best be described as unrepresentative democracy.

Johnson's appeal to his base rests heavily on his enthusiastic comments about a 'no-deal' Brexit, a kamikaze policy that would devastate Britain's economy and produce a state of emergency for basic civil infrastructure, such as the supply of medicines. It would, however, signal a complete rejection of the authority of Brussels, which is why Johnson toys with it. The fact that a clear majority of the public opposes the idea is, for now, irrelevant. More disturbingly, new polling suggests that Conservative Party members are now so fixated on Brexit that they believe it is worth doing at almost any cost – even if it leads to Northern Ireland or Scotland leaving the United Kingdom, 'significant damage to the UK economy' or, most strikingly, the destruction of the Conservative Party.[4] For the next few weeks, the most influential force in British politics is a fanatical sect.

How did Britain reach this extraordinary situation? A plausible part of the explanation is that the Conservative Party has been heavily infiltrated by supporters of Nigel Farage, whose new Brexit Party took more than a third of the vote in May's European Parliament elections, energised by the fact that Britain did not leave the European Union on the scheduled date of 29 March.

Last August, Arron Banks, a major UKIP funder over the years and backer of the xenophobic Leave.EU campaign, wrote an op-ed for *The Times* titled 'Join Tories and unseat the traitor Theresa'. It's hard to know for certain how many people have followed Banks's advice, but Faragism has clearly penetrated the Conservative Party. What's more, the majority of Johnson's supporters in the membership joined the party *after* the 2016 referendum. The party also appears to have experienced a surge in membership of around 30 per cent since last summer, when confidence in May's Brexit deal started to plummet.

Pockets of deep resentment towards governing 'elites' are a feature of most liberal democracies today, to which there are a range of possible responses. What's different in Britain is the collision between its old-fashioned, unwritten constitution and the exceptional drama of Brexit, which has become a Trojan Horse through which nationalist, anti-establishment rage is being channelled directly into the corridors of power. For years, the case for reforming Britain's constitution, to ensure that parties and Parliament are more representative of the public, has been viewed as a somewhat academic topic, never urgent enough to demand much attention. Not any more. For the time being, Johnson has said enough to reassure the Conservative members that he will govern with the same xenophobic bravado that he has always expressed in his journalism. But if Johnson's personality offers one glimmer of hope, it's that he's never shown any indication of holding principles, and is entirely relaxed about letting people down.

England's New Rentier Alliance

It's plausible that Boris Johnson could win a workable majority in an election, sometime in the next six months, and this is obviously something he would do if he possibly could. If he did, who and what would he represent? It's easy to say 'Leavers' or 'English nationalists' and leave it at that. But I wonder if there is an economic formation at work too. There is a sub-set of the Leave vote that appears to have hardened over the past two years, becoming more fixated on 'no deal', and less willing to brook compromise. Surveys suggest that support for 'no deal' is clustered among older voters who report that they are financially secure.[5] We also know from those notorious polls of Conservative Party members that they view Brexit as more important than economic prosperity and the Union. This group is scattered across rural England, and elected the current prime minister.

We can also look at the funders for the Leave campaign and Johnson's leadership bid, who overlap heavily. These consist of maverick entrepreneurs (the bosses of JCB and Wetherspoons), private equity barons and hedge fund managers. This is decentralised, disruptive, disorganised, private capital, that looks at the likes of Johnson and Farage as kindred spirits in the project of injecting a bit of chaos into the liberal economic system. Regardless of how much agency we attribute to hedge funds (and there are various theories), it is clear that only the most fleet-footed, liquid, nimble type of capital can look at Brexit as an opportunity, while firms that rely heavily on fixed capital (such as car manufacturers) see it as a nightmare. This is capital that is never far from the exit.

I think we can therefore look at the new conservative coalition as an alliance of rentiers. The 'no deal' supporters are not classic rentiers, in the form of monopolists or exploiters of unproductive capital. However, they are at a point in life where they have paid off their mortgages, and are living off the assets held by pension funds. They are *worth something*, independently of what they do. This is the generation that enthusiastically backed Margaret Thatcher in their early working lives, witnessed Blairism and the booming of metropolitan multiculturalism with growing unease, and perhaps felt a rising resentment towards the international elite that was making the serious money in London, while convincing themselves (with the help of the *Daily Express*, the *Daily Mail* and the *Daily Telegraph*) that London is now a foreign city (a fiction that Johnson cynically endorsed in his leadership campaign).[6]

What this group shares with the Johnson and Farage backers is a lack of any immediate interest in labour markets or productive capitalism. What's the worst that could happen from the perspective of these interests? Inflation or a stock market slump would certainly harm them, but they may have forgotten that these things are even possible. Jeremy Corbyn terrifies them even more than Remain, as they believe he will tax capital, gifts and inheritance into oblivion. Where productivity gains are no longer sought, the goal becomes defending private wealth and keeping it in the family. This is a logic that unites the international oligarch and the comfortable *Telegraph*-reading retiree in Hampshire. The mentality is one of pulling up the drawbridge, and cashing in your chips.

This suggests that Johnson-Farage is a symptom of prolonged financialisation, in which capital pulls increasingly towards unproductive investments, relying on balance-sheet manipulation, negative interest rates and liquidity for its returns (aided substantially by quantitative easing over the past decade). To put that more starkly, these are seriously morbid symptoms, in which all productive opportunities have already been seized, no new ideas or technologies are likely, and there are no new spheres of social or environmental life left to exploit and commodify. These are socially nihilistic interests whose only concern with the future involves their children and grandchildren, but otherwise believe that everything good is in the past. The term 'late capitalism' has been over used, but this certainly feels like *very* late capitalism.

From this perspective, the present looks like the outcome of past investments. If you're rich, it's because you invested well thirty or forty years ago. You don't owe anything to anyone, and have no obligation to invest anything more for the future. It's your money, because of the time that elapsed while it was accumulating. The extreme manifestation of this nostalgic nihilism is Arron Banks, who is the decaying face of Harry Enfield's Thatcherite 'loadsamoney' character, now living off the proceeds of his previous investments, while continuing to troll people about how little he cares about society. The financial troll uses his money to smash things up, as a type of conspicuous consumption: a way, as Thorstein Veblen argued, of showing how much money you can afford to waste, and how insulated you are from the consequences of your actions.[7] For men such as Tim Martin, boss of Wetherspoons, backing 'no deal' is a way of signalling that you're rich enough to take a haircut of a few million off your assets.

What of the remaining 70 per cent of the population, who are firmly opposed to an ultra-hard or 'no-deal' Brexit? It includes conventional business lobbies, who care about international supply chains, regulatory stability, skills and support for innovation. These are the interests that were exceptionally well served under New Labour and by the

European Union. It also includes those who own nothing, and are vulnerable to week-by-week changes in their income and the cost of food. Finally, it includes most people under the age of fifty who still have hopes and expectations for the future, and relate to that future via the conventions of work, careers, debt and investment. Many of these people care deeply about climate change, far more than about Brexit.

Johnson, Farage and 'no deal' offer nothing to this majority whatsoever. That is a vulnerability, and there are reasons to suspect that the Liberal Democrats could pose just as much of a threat as Labour, if they become identified as the sole representatives of pro-business, Blairite modernity. There is also the not insignificant chunk of Conservative voters who support Remain and would rather Jeremy Hunt was prime minister right now. But until some of the political representatives of that 70 per cent construct *some kind* of coalition, and identify the language and overlapping policies that it shares (in spite of its deep heterogeneity), then the alliance of the nostalgic rentiers will succeed.

The Johnson Press

Over the course of Boris Johnson's leadership campaign, Britain has been treated to a fresh media spectacle, marking a new low in the slow decline of an autonomous press. The *Daily Telegraph*, which has employed Boris Johnson off and on for over thirty years, and currently pays him £275,000 a year as a columnist, has put its full editorial and journalistic resource behind his bid to become leader of the

Conservative Party, and therefore prime minister. Beside the constant trickle of op-eds praising his character and political judgement, the paper published an opinion poll on the morning of his leadership campaign launch, predicting he would win a majority of 140 in a general election, and has converted its front page into a type of campaign leaflet, full of flattering photos and slogans.

At best, this is distasteful and creepy. But is it dangerous? On its own, it is not substantially different from the way the newspapers fell behind Tony Blair in the late 1990s and early 2000s, or the *Daily Mail* briefly worked for Theresa May in 2016–17. But its broader context points to something more worrying than those precedents, with immediate echoes of what's taking place on the other side of the Atlantic. The sound of journalists being booed at Johnson's launch event should be enough to raise concerns of something Trumpian going on.

The rising intimacy between party machinery and the press (and hence, the declining public trust in both) is often blamed on New Labour, and Alastair Campbell particularly. Winning Rupert Murdoch's support for Labour was viewed as a strategic triumph for Campbell and Blair, and an act of cynical deference by their critics. But it's worth remembering that these doyens of 'spin' only placed so much emphasis on pleasing the press because they'd been so bruised by Murdoch et al. in the late 1980s and early '90s. Spin, as we came to know it, was born under duress. New Labour might be accused of cynicism and superficiality in their fixation on headlines, but that fixation was a result of them deeming the press to be so dangerous. Blair, it is often forgotten, dedicated one of his last speeches to lambasting the 'feral beasts' of the media. The relationship between Downing Street and Fleet Street was, at best, one of détente (Blair's growing personal camaraderie with Murdoch did nothing to help Gordon Brown).

The past decade has seen the Conservative Party develop a far closer relationship to the press that goes well beyond image management and spin. While Blair appointed a former journalist as his spin doctor, David Cameron put a former *Times* journalist (Michael Gove) and former *Telegraph* journalist (Johnson) in his cabinet, and a *Times* columnist and leader writer (Danny Finkelstein) in the House of Lords. Gove's wife, Sarah Vine, was also a *Times* columnist until 2013. The relationship between Cameronism and journalism worked both ways, as demonstrated when George Osborne was appointed editor of the *Evening Standard* despite no journalistic experience whatsoever. Johnson had to abandon his *Telegraph* column during his woeful tenure as foreign secretary, but continued to use the newspaper to outline his views on Brexit and other matters, who reported them gushingly as 'exclusives'.

Johnson's impending premiership has to be understood in this context, one in which journalists become politicians, and politicians become journalists. Rather than policies being developed and then 'spun' for media consumption, power becomes held by the storytellers themselves. But this is only one part of the story of how we reached the nadir of journalists being booed for failing to endorse a political candidate. The other part concerns technology.

By-passing journalism

As is now well understood, digital platforms have transformed the possibilities for political communication, by-passing traditional channels, and allowing political campaigns to target and address potential voters without the mediation of journalists, editors or broadcasting regulations. The democratic shocks of 2016 have been partly credited to Facebook's power to connect campaigns (and carefully tailored campaign messages) directly with individuals, without any broader public awareness. This turns all campaigning into a form of 'dog-whistling', in which political messages circumvent the traditional, analogue public sphere.

One consequence of this is that the public (and even rival campaigns) don't know what messages are being used or who they're being aimed at. Targeted messaging appears to produce particular volatility where it is used to persuade non-voters to vote for the first time, as occurred with the EU referendum. But another consequence is that channels now exist through which to observe, criticise and dismiss journalists and the 'mainstream media'. Trump famously uses Twitter to attack CNN, the *New York Times* and any other news agencies that report things he doesn't like. Far-right activists and conspiracy theorists use YouTube and Facebook to accuse particular news channels of conspiring to cover up the truth. The claim that journalists are 'enemies of the people' can now be distributed as easily as news itself.

This has contributed to a situation in which press conferences and broadcast interviews are now inessential. Theresa May's fateful 2017 election campaign intuited this, but acted

on it half-heartedly, seeking to control her public engage-
ments sufficiently to look paranoid and robotic, but not
enough to avoid that impression leaking out to the electorate. Johnson's campaign team is clearly going to make no
such mistake, and it's here that we enter Trumpian territory.

Johnson has famously given no broadcast interview
over this campaign season, and has avoided live debates.
Clearly, he has no real incentive to participate: he simply
needs to outline a policy idea in the *Telegraph*, or make some
implausibly bold statement in a newspaper interview, and
it immediately gets repeated by broadcasters. The *Sunday
Times* has become a willing accomplice to media-sceptic
demagogues, running successive fawning interviews with
Trump and Johnson, and producing front-page splashes
('Trump: send in Farage and go for no-deal'; 'Johnson:
The £39bn is ours') which might just as easily have been
tweets from the men themselves. These too get reported by
the BBC.

The Johnson launch event was a chilling spectacle for
anyone who hopes he will be held to account by the press.
Immediately announcing that he would take just six questions, he did at least manage to avoid the temptation to take
all six from the *Daily Telegraph* and the *Sunday Times*. But
the performance was troubling nonetheless. The political
editor of Sky News, Beth Rigby, attempted to ask a question about his 'character', which he immediately pretended
to mis-hear as 'parrot', to much mirth. While Trump uses
anger, and Johnson uses humour, the effect is the same: the
journalistic space shifts from one of enquiry and testimony
to one of performance and audience frisson. Humour is

doing something very significant in our digital public sphere in helping political leaders to evade criticism.

Rigby persevered with her question about Johnson's Islamophobic remarks which compared veiled Muslim women to 'letterboxes'. It was here that his massed ranks of ERG supporters – high on the feeling of collective irresponsibility, like a Thatcher-themed stag-do in Riga – began to boo. Rigby had overstepped the mark by bringing unwelcome facts into the room. The booing was later defended by *Telegraph* columnist Allison Pearson, who tweeted at BBC editor, Laura Kuenssberg:

> The 'jeers' at Boris's launch were for Sky News's Beth Rigby and her editorialising question. Much like yours, shamefully biased. If @BBCnews continues to distort and withhold information from viewers there will be trouble.

In this tweet alone, one can see a worst-case scenario emerging. Criticism of Johnson will be called 'bias'. The BBC will be accused of 'withholding information', and threats will follow. Who's to say that Kuenssberg or Rigby will definitely be invited to Downing Street press conferences under a Johnson premiership? That might sound hysterical, but the precedent is being set in Washington DC.

This is a qualitatively different state of affairs from the one masterminded by Campbell and Blair. The vision outlined by Pearson is one shared by Nigel Farage and the 'Yellow Vests' on the street who mobilise behind Stephen Yaxley-Lennon. If individual journalists pose difficult questions about a 'no-deal Brexit' (and its figureheads), then they are 'biased' Remainers. Carl Schmitt's 'friend–enemy' distinction enters the press conference, and the leader only speaks to his friends.

Social media is a crucial ingredient in this, converting press conferences from a normal (indeed necessary) feature of constitutional democracy into a luxury, to be enjoyed or else dispensed with. What Trump demonstrates (and what May's team couldn't quite deal with) is that there is no symbiotic relationship between journalism and power any longer. Either the distinction between journalism and executive power dissolves altogether (as has happened with Fox News and the White House, and could soon be witnessed with the *Daily Telegraph* and Downing Street), or else politicians speak over the heads of the professional media altogether.

As important as media transformations have been, it's unlikely that Britain would have reached this juncture if it weren't for Brexit. It is Brexit that has injected what Schmitt termed 'political theology' into British politics, introducing questions of 'sovereignty' that are not amenable to empirical or reasoned discussion. It is Brexit, with the aid of social media, that has turned mass fury upon those institutions which hold up a mirror to society – not only Parliament, but experts and reporters. And it is Brexit that has provided Johnson with his long-sought opportunity to perform his pointless egotism on the highest stage in the land.

American journalists have struggled to know how to respond to Trump's behaviour. The *New York Times* and *Washington Post* have set out a grand vision of hostile truthtelling, which fuels Trump's persecution complex and gives him a steady flow of material to confirm that the media has it in for him. Johnson might welcome similar treatment, although the BBC would find it politically difficult to go for him (and for hard Brexit) in the same way that US news attacks Trump.

But there is an opportunity for journalistic collectivism and solidarity here. The BBC and the sceptical papers need to do what they can to avoid cooperating with Johnson's messaging. An 'exclusive' Johnson column in the *Telegraph* or interview with the *Sunday Times* needn't be headline news. An opinion poll published in the paper that pays Johnson £275,000 a year should be reported as internal to the race, rather than an objective picture of it. Above all, if on the rare occasions Johnson confronts journalistic scrutiny, there is intimidation of any sort, every member of the press should walk out leaving his tribe to fluff his ego undisturbed.

The Blizzard of Lies

Politics has never been a pursuit that requires total honesty. Nor, historically, has it been a vocation that scientists or other kinds of expert are drawn to. The New Labour era, which produced an elite career escalator linking university, think-tank, ministerial advice, Parliament and finally government, was an anomaly in the longer sweep of things. The reason there are so many mechanisms in place to remind powerful people of the actual facts of matters – mechanisms that include quangos and policy research institutes and publicly funded broadcasters – is that we assume they need constant reminding. A functioning constitution should be able to cope with the odd charlatan and bullshit artist, steering them gently away from the levers of power like a friend removing car keys from a drunk.

When we say that someone is 'good with words', we don't mean they are reliable in how they relate them to things and deeds. On the contrary, the most brilliant rhetoricians or storytellers are those who can conjure an escape from the tedious constraints of the facts or past promises. However much the media pursues the question of Boris Johnson's 'character', we shouldn't kid ourselves that politics has ever been a truthfulness contest.

How much worse can things get? Quite a bit, it turns out. If politics has always attracted and to some extent rewarded the liar, the effect of Brexit on public life is that there is now a penalty attached to speaking the truth. The Conservative leadership contest is a curious spectator sport (save for the 160,000 electors with Conservative Party membership cards) in which the first contestant to accept reality is the loser. Words have now broken completely free of their factual moorings; Johnson and Jeremy Hunt seem committed to touring the nation and its television studios misreporting and misdescribing the economic, legal and political realities that will confront the next prime minister. To do otherwise would be an act of surrender.

Things have been drifting in this direction since the 2016 referendum campaign, with its infamous lie that 'we send the EU £350 million a week'. Hardline Brexiteers now revel in their disregard for the statements of experts and fact-checkers, whom they lump together with the BBC, Channel 4, Whitehall and universities as part of a Remain tendency in public life. The beauty of 'sovereignty' as a political ideal is its metaphysical character, which evades efforts by economists and civil servants to pin it down, and seems to release political speech from the straitjacket of verifiable evidence.

Whole new vistas of political and cultural possibility seem to open up as a result. The political liar 'is an actor by nature', Hannah Arendt wrote. 'He says what is not so because he wants things to be different from what they are – that is, he wants to change the world … Our ability to lie – but not necessarily our ability to tell the truth – belongs among the few obvious, demonstrable data that confirm human freedom.'[8] Freedom is what this is all about. The complaint that 'you can't say anything any more' is often heard as a grudge against 'political correctness', but the yearning to be able to *say anything* can just as easily find expression in support for the leader who will do precisely that, regardless of evidence.

From this perspective, the Remainer fixation on facts appears like a form of verbal constipation, to which Johnson's gleeful freewheeling serves as the remedy. Note that the quality Johnson's fans most applaud in him is cheerfulness, something Theresa May was never going to offer, suggesting that she may have missed the point of Brexit all along. The 2019 summer has taken on a carnivalesque quality; normal constraints around public speech have been suspended for the duration of a truth jubilee.

As this 'cheerfulness' is ratcheted up, the freedom to 'say anything' starts to engulf an expanding array of policy domains. With the leadership contest entering its final weeks, the same can-say attitude has been directed towards fiscal policy. Johnson and Hunt are now offering tax cuts and public spending increases which, by any account, would add tens of billions to the annual deficit (Labour claims that Johnson's plans would add £57 billion, Hunt's £43 billion) – when the vital necessity of reducing the deficit had previously been the Conservative justification for austerity.

Johnson has promised to end public-sector pay freezes. To get Britain through a 'no-deal' scenario, Hunt is invoking a positively Rooseveltian fiscal spirit, tweeting: 'We spent just over £1 trillion bailing out the banks after the financial crisis. So if we did it for the bankers then why wouldn't we now do what is needed for our fishermen and our farmers?' Never one to be outdone in rhetorical hyperbole, Nigel Farage has started fleshing out a Brexit Party policy programme with a promise of £200 billion (more than the entire budget of the NHS and schools put together) to be invested in non-London regions.

An interesting subplot in this festival of Keynesian ideas is the status of broadband access. One of Johnson's first policy announcements was to offer 'full fibre to every home in the land' by 2025, which civil engineers consider utterly unrealistic (the government's current 'aspiration' to deliver it by 2033 is very optimistic). Farage has also fixated on faster broadband nationwide, plus free and fast wifi on buses and trains outside London. There was a time when the internet was identified with the 'global village' and hipster start-up culture; now it has become a key symbol and rallying point of non-metropolitan nationhood. The Farage-Johnson fantasy, it seems, is to weaken the cultural power of the large cities and university towns (those splodges of Remain on the Brexit map of England), and with it the influence of the BBC and Channel 4. Who really needs public service broadcasters in this high-speed internet future? Let a million YouTube channels bloom.

Loose talk is infectious and addictive. It begins with a dodgy claim on the side of a bus, and before you know it you've promised a spending spree so lavish that John McDonnell is accusing you of being 'reckless'. But something significant has happened along the way that may cause particular concern to traditional Conservative sympathisers in the business and financial sectors. The claim that politicians are 'liars' can encompass two quite different kinds of lie. The first concerns facts – that is, things that have verifiably happened in the past. The '£350 million' was this kind of lie: it excluded the money Britain had received back every week. It is this kind of lying that Donald Trump engages in compulsively, denying the public record, disowning past statements. It consists in a refusal to be bound by empirical data or by witnesses.

The second concerns broken promises, which is what many assume will happen once Johnson or Hunt enters Downing Street and is finally confronted by the realities of Brussels and Treasury bureaucracy. But until that future arrives, promises aren't really lies so much as dubious pledges. What's happened to British politics over the past three years is that, on discovering that it's possible to lie about the past and get away with it, Conservatives now speak about the future as if there won't really be one. Dishonesty about facts bleeds into dishonesty about intentions and prospects.

One might imagine that the first type of lie – the Trumpian one – is the more egregious. After all, if it's an established *fact* that Europe's trade surplus with the US is $101 billion, it's surely monstrous to claim that it's $151 billion. Such mendacity does a fundamental violence to the relationship between language and the world. But business and financial interests have often been far more worried by the second type of dishonesty, the failure to keep one's word. Frankly, investors don't really care about lies plastered on buses or asserted about the size of the crowd at an inauguration. If the next prime minister insists that the global climate cooled down in 2018 or that the European Union banned bendy bananas, it's of no great concern to the CBI. It is when politicians start to talk big about the future that financiers get antsy.

Because investment is a future-oriented activity, one of the main threats that democracy poses to capitalism is that cast-iron policies, promises and rules can be tossed aside at any moment. It isn't just voters who worry about politicians' honesty: businesses worry that political words deployed as mere rhetoric, to win favour in the short term, can never reliably operate as a constraint. This problem has been especially acute in the era of neoliberal globali-sation that emerged after the 1970s, as nation states have constantly sought to reassure international investors that they will stick to predictable regulatory, monetary and fis-cal frameworks. Various instruments have been invented to achieve this, from central bank independence, which removes monetary policy from the domain of democratic politics, to the 'stability and growth pact' that has limited

European Union member states' fiscal freedoms since 1999, to Gordon Brown's self-imposed 'Golden Rule', which stipulated public borrowing limits.

Business investors can cope with various models of capitalism, involving a wide range of tax rates, corporate governance systems and regulatory frameworks. What they can't cope with is perpetual uncertainty. When political promises no longer hold their value over time, the value of a nation's money will eventually suffer the same fate: inflation and devaluation are the consequence. (At its simplest, the neoliberal diagnosis of 1970s inflation was that too much democracy had led politicians and employers to make more promises than they were economically capable of honouring.) Contrary to everything George Osborne led us to believe, it isn't deficit spending as such that threatens economic stability: it's the fact that Johnson's words offer scarcely any clue as to what he plans to *do*.

If the Conservative Party is about to draw a line under the era of austerity in such exuberant fashion it ought to be surprising. Then again, the right has often been less neurotic about prudence than the left (especially in the US); the right knows, after all, that it doesn't have to work as hard as the left to win the trust of capital. But in the present atmosphere, few of Johnson or Hunt's pledges seem likely to survive very far into the autumn. Spending commitments are being let off like fireworks, lighting up the night sky for the immediate pleasure of the 160,000 voters. Compared to Johnson's 'do or die' promise to depart the EU on 31 October regardless of whether a deal is in place, pledging a few billion here and there is just noise.

But all this does pose worrying questions about what kind of democratic government will exist once the UK has got through the next six months of uncertainty. Who or what will voters and businesses be placing their trust in when political speech has finally been reconfigured as mere mood music, to be used to soothe or excite, but never to constrain? Politics could become riven by a kind of 'front-stage/back-stage' duality, fronted by 'cheerful' figures speaking the language of sovereignty, while brushing aside the details of policy and spending for others to deal with. Like the reality of austerity, the reality of Brexit will become visible at some stage. But who's to say that its cheerleaders will be prepared to recognise it as such?

Why Everyone Hates the 'Mainstream Media'

We live in a time of political fury and hardening cultural divides. But if there is one thing on which virtually everyone is agreed, it is that the news and information we receive is biased. Every second of every day, someone is complaining about bias, in everything from the latest movie reviews to sports commentary to the BBC's coverage of Brexit. These complaints and controversies take up a growing share of public discussion. Much of the outrage that floods social media, occasionally leaking into opinion columns and broadcast interviews, is not simply a reaction to events themselves, but to the way in which they are reported and framed. The 'mainstream media' is the principal focal point for this anger. Journalists and broadcasters who purport to be neutral are a constant object of scrutiny and derision, whenever they appear to let their personal views slip. The work of journalists involves an increasing amount of unscripted, real-time discussion, which provides an occasionally troubling window into their thinking.

But this is not simply an anti-journalist sentiment. A similar fury can just as easily descend on a civil servant or independent expert whenever their veneer of neutrality seems to crack, apparently revealing prejudices underneath. Sometimes a report or claim is dismissed as biased or inaccurate for the simple reason that it is unwelcome: to a Brexiteer, every bad economic forecast is just another case of the so-called project fear. A sense that the game is rigged now fuels public debate. This mentality spans the entire political spectrum and pervades societies around the world. One survey shows that the majority of people globally believe their society is broken and their economy is rigged.[9] Both the left and the right feel misrepresented and misunderstood by political institutions and the media, but the anger is shared by many in the liberal centre, who believe that populists have gamed the system to harvest more attention than they deserve. Outrage at 'mainstream' institutions has become a mass sentiment.

This spirit of indignation was once the natural property of the left, which has long resented the establishment bias of the press. But in the present culture war, the right points to the universities, the BBC and the civil service as institutions that twist our basic understanding of reality to suit their own ends. Everyone can point to evidence that justifies their outrage. This arms race in cultural analysis is unwinnable.

This is not as simple as distrust. The appearance of digital platforms, smartphones and the ubiquitous surveillance they enable has ushered in a new public mood that is instinctively suspicious of anyone claiming to describe reality in a fair and objective fashion. It is a mindset that begins with legitimate curiosity about what motivates a given media story, but which ends in a Trumpian refusal to accept any mainstream or official account of the world. We can all probably locate ourselves somewhere on this spectrum, between the curiosity of the engaged citizen and the corrosive cynicism of the climate denier. The question is whether this mentality is doing us any good, either individually or collectively.

Public life has become like a play whose audience is unwilling to suspend disbelief. Any utterance by a public figure can be unpicked in search of its ulterior motive. As cynicism grows, even judges, the supposedly neutral upholders of the law, are publicly accused of personal bias. Once doubt descends on public life, people become increasingly dependent on their own experiences and their own beliefs about how the world really works. One effect of this is that facts no longer seem to matter (the phenomenon misleadingly dubbed 'post-truth'). But the crises of democracy and of truth are one and the same: individuals are increasingly suspicious of the 'official' stories they are being told, and expect to witness things for themselves.

On one level, heightened scepticism towards the establishment is a welcome development. A more media-literate and critical citizenry ought to be less easy for the powerful to manipulate. It may even represent a victory for the type of cultural critique pioneered by intellectuals such as Pierre

Bourdieu and Stuart Hall in the 1970s and '80s, revealing the injustices embedded in everyday cultural expressions and interactions. But it is possible to have too much scepticism. How exactly do we distinguish this critical mentality from that of the conspiracy theorist, who is convinced that they alone have seen through the official version of events? Or to turn the question around, how might it be possible to recognise the most flagrant cases of bias in the behaviour of reporters and experts, but nevertheless to accept that what they say is often a reasonable depiction of the world?

It is tempting to blame the internet, populists or foreign trolls for flooding our otherwise rational society with lies. But this underestimates the scale of the technological and philosophical transformations that are underway. The single biggest change in our public sphere is that we now have an unimaginable excess of news and content, where once we had scarcity. Suddenly, the analogue channels and professions we depended on for our knowledge of the world have come to seem partial, slow and dispensable. And yet, contrary to initial hype surrounding big data, the explosion of information available to us is making it harder, not easier, to achieve consensus on truth. As the quantity of information increases, the need to pick out bite-size pieces of content rises accordingly. In this radically sceptical age, questions of where to look, what to focus on and who to trust are ones that we increasingly seek to answer for ourselves, without the help of intermediaries. This is a liberation of sorts, but it is also at the heart of our deteriorating confidence in public institutions.

The data deluge

The current threat to democracy is often seen to emanate from new forms of propaganda, with the implication that lies are being deliberately fed to a naive and over-emotional public. The simultaneous rise of populist parties and digital platforms has triggered well-known anxieties regarding the fate of truth in democratic societies. Fake news and internet echo chambers are believed to manipulate and ghettoise certain communities, for shadowy ends. Key groups – millennials or the white working class, say – are accused of being easily persuadable, thanks to their excessive sentimentality.

This diagnosis exaggerates old-fashioned threats while overlooking new phenomena. Over-reliant on analogies to twentieth-century totalitarianism, it paints the present moment as a moral conflict between truth and lies, with an unthinking public passively consuming the results. But our relationship to information and news is now entirely different: it has become an active and critical one, deeply suspicious of the official line. Nowadays, everyone is engaged in spotting and rebutting propaganda of one kind or another, curating our news feeds, attacking the framing of the other side and consciously resisting manipulation. In some ways, we have become *too* concerned with truth, to the point where we can no longer agree on it. The very institutions that might have once brought controversies to an end are under constant fire for their compromises and biases.

The threat of misinformation and propaganda should not be denied. As the scholars Yochai Benkler, Robert Faris and Hal Roberts have shown in their book *Network Propaganda*, there is now a self-sustaining information ecosystem on the American right, through which conspiracy theories and untruths get recycled, between Breitbart, Fox News, talk radio and social media.[10] Meanwhile, the anti-vax movement is becoming a serious public health problem across the world, aided by the online circulation of conspiracy theories and pseudo-science. This is a situation where simple misinformation poses a serious threat to society.

But away from these eye-catching cases, things look less clear-cut. The majority of people in northern Europe still regularly encounter mainstream news and information. Britain is a long way from the US experience, thanks principally to the presence of the BBC, which, for all its faults, still performs a basic function in providing a common informational experience. It is treated as a primary source of news by 60 per cent of people in the UK. Even 42 per cent of Brexit Party and UKIP voters get their news from the BBC. The panic surrounding echo chambers and so-called filter bubbles is largely groundless. If we think of an echo chamber as a sealed environment, which only circulates opinions and facts that are agreeable to its participants, it is a rather implausible phenomenon. Research by the Oxford Internet Institute suggests that just 8 per cent of the UK public are at risk of becoming trapped in such a clique.[11]

Trust in the media is low, but this entrenched scepticism long predates the internet or contemporary populism. From the *Sun*'s lies about Hillsborough to the BBC's failure to expose Jimmy Savile as early as they might have, to the fevered enthusiasm for the Iraq War that gripped much of Fleet Street, the British public has had plenty of good reasons to distrust journalists. Even so, the number of people in the UK who trust journalists to tell the truth has actually risen slightly since the 1980s.[12]

What, then, has changed? The key thing is that the elites of government and the media have lost their monopoly over the provision of information, but retain their prominence in the public eye. They have become more like celebrities, anti-heroes or figures in a reality TV show. And digital platforms now provide a public space in which to identify and rake over the flaws, biases and falsehoods of mainstream institutions. The result is increasingly sceptical citizens, each seeking to manage their media diet, checking up on individual journalists in order to resist the pernicious influence of the establishment.

There are clear and obvious benefits to this, where it allows hateful and manipulative journalism to be called out. But it also generates a mood of outrage, which is far more focused on denouncing bad and biased reporting than on defending the alternative. Across the political spectrum, we are increasingly distracted and enraged by what our adversaries deem important and how they frame it. Often it is not the media's lies that provoke the greatest fury online, but the discovery that an important event has been ignored or downplayed, or conversely elevated unduly. While it is true that arguments rage over dodgy facts and figures (concerning climate change or the details of Britain's trading relations), many of the most bitter controversies of our news cycle concern the framing and weighting of different issues and how they are reported, rather than the facts of what actually happened.

The problem we face is not, then, that certain people are

oblivious to the 'mainstream media', or are victims of fake news, but that we are all seeking to see through the veneer of facts and information provided to us by public institutions. Facts and official reports are no longer the end of the story. Such scepticism is healthy and, in many ways, the just deserts of an establishment that has been caught twisting the truth too many times. But political problems arise once we turn against all representations and framings of reality, on the basis that they are compromised and biased – as if some purer, unmediated access to the truth might be possible instead. This is a seductive, but misleading ideal.

Journalism without journalists

Every human culture throughout history has developed ways to record experiences and events, allowing them to endure. From early modern times, liberal societies have developed a wide range of institutions and professions whose work ensures that events do not simply pass without trace or public awareness. Newspapers and broadcasters share reports, photographs and footage of things that have happened in politics, business, society and culture. Court documents and the Hansard parliamentary reports provide records of what has been said in law courts and in Parliament. Systems of accounting, auditing and economics help to establish basic facts about what takes place in businesses and markets.

Traditionally, it is through these systems, which are grounded in written testimonies and public statements, that we have learned what is going on in the world. But in the past twenty years, this patchwork of record-keeping has been supplemented and threatened by a radically different system, which is transforming the nature of empirical evidence and memory. One term for this is 'big data', which highlights the exponential growth in the quantity of data that societies create, thanks to digital technologies.

The reason there is so much data today is that more and more of our social lives are mediated digitally. Internet browsers, smartphones, social media platforms, smart cards and every other smart interface record every move we make. Whether or not we are conscious of it, we are constantly leaving traces of our activities, no matter how trivial. But it is not the escalating quantity of data that constitutes the radical change. Something altogether new has occurred that distinguishes today's society from previous epochs. In the past, recording devices were principally trained upon events that were already acknowledged as important. Journalists did not just report news, but determined what counted as newsworthy. TV crews turned up at events that were deemed of national significance. The rest of us kept our cameras for noteworthy occasions, such as holidays and parties.

The ubiquity of digital technology has thrown all of this up in the air. Things no longer need to be judged 'important' to be captured. Consciously, we photograph events and record experiences regardless of their importance. Unconsciously, we leave a trace of our behaviour every time we swipe a smart card, address Amazon's Alexa or touch our phone. For the first time in human history, recording now happens by default, and the question of significance is addressed separately.

This shift has prompted an unrealistic set of expectations regarding the possibilities for human knowledge. As many of the original evangelists of big data liked to claim, when everything is being recorded, our knowledge of the world no longer needs to be mediated by professionals, experts, institutions and theories. Instead, they argued, the data can simply 'speak for itself'. Patterns will emerge, traces will come to light. This holds out the prospect of some purer truth than the one presented to us by professional editors or trained experts. As the Australian surveillance scholar Mark Andrejevic has brilliantly articulated, this is a fantasy of a truth unpolluted by any deliberate human intervention – the ultimate in scientific objectivity.

Andrejevic argues that the rise of this fantasy coincides with a growing impatience at the efforts of reporters and experts to frame reality in meaningful ways. He writes that 'we might describe the contemporary media moment – and its characteristic attitude of sceptical savviness regarding the contrivance of representation – as one that implicitly embraces the ideal of framelessness'.[13] From this perspective, every controversy can in principle be settled thanks to the vast trove of data – CCTV, records of digital activity and so on – now available to us. Reality in its totality is being recorded, and reporters and officials look dismally compromised by comparison.

One way in which a seemingly frameless media has transformed public life over recent years is in the elevation of photography and video as arbiters of truth, as opposed to written testimony or numbers. 'Pics or it didn't happen' is a jokey barb sometimes thrown at social media users when they share some unlikely experience. It is often a single image that seems to capture the truth of an event, only now there are cameras everywhere. No matter how many times it is disproven, the notion that 'the camera doesn't lie' has a peculiar hold over our imaginations. In a society of blanket CCTV and smartphones, there are more cameras than people, and the torrent of data adds to the sense that the truth is somewhere amid the deluge, ignored by mainstream accounts. The central demand of this newly sceptical public is 'so show me'.

This transformation in our recording equipment is responsible for much of the outrage directed at those formerly tasked with describing the world. The rise of blanket surveillance technologies has paradoxical effects, raising expectations for objective knowledge to unrealistic levels, and then provoking fury when those in the public eye do not meet them.

On the one hand, data science appears to make the question of objective truth easier to settle. The slow and imperfect institutions of social science and journalism can be circumvented, and we can get directly to reality itself, unpolluted by human bias. Surely, in this age of mass data capture, the truth will become undeniable. On the other hand, as the quantity of data becomes overwhelming – greater than human intelligence can comprehend – our ability to agree on the nature of reality seems to be declining. Once everything is, in principle, recordable, disputes heat up regarding what counts as significant in the first place. It turns out that the 'frames' that journalists and experts use to reduce and organise information are indispensable to its coherence and meaning.

What we are discovering is that, once the limitations on data capture are removed, there are escalating opportunities for conflict over the nature of reality. Every time a mainstream media agency reports the news, they can instantly be met with the retort: but what about this other event, in another time and another place, that you failed to report? What about the bits you left out? What about the other voters in the town you didn't talk to? When editors judge the relative importance of stories, they now confront a panoply of alternative judgements. Where records are abundant, fights break out over relevance and meaning.

Professional editors have always faced the challenge of reducing long interviews to short consumable chunks or discarding the majority of photos or text. Editing is largely a question of what to throw away. This necessitates value judgements, that readers and audiences once had little option but to trust. Now, however, the question of which image or sentence is truly significant opens irresolvable arguments. One person's offcut is another person's revealing nugget.

Political agendas can be pursued this way, including cynical ones aimed at painting one's opponents in the worst possible light. An absurd or extreme voice can be represented as typical of a political movement (known as 'nutpicking'). Taking quotes out of context is one of the most disruptive of online ploys, which provokes far more fury than simple insults. Rather than deploying lies or 'fake news', it messes with the significance of data, taking the fact that someone did say or write something, but violating their intended meaning. No doubt professional journalists have always descended to such tactics from time to time, but now we are all at it, provoking a vicious circle of misrepresentation.

Then consider the status of photography and video. It is

not just that photographic evidence can be manipulated to mislead, but that questions will always survive regarding camera angle and context. What happened before or after a camera started rolling? What was outside the shot? These questions provoke suspicion, often with good reason.

The most historic example of such a controversy predates digital media. The Zapruder film, which captured the assassination of John F. Kennedy, became the most scrutinised piece of footage in history. The film helped spawn countless conspiracy theories, with individual frames becoming the focus of competing theories as to what they reveal. The difficulty of completely squaring any narrative with a photographic image is a philosophical one as much as anything, and the Zapruder film gave a glimpse of the sorts of media disputes that have become endemic now cameras are a ubiquitous part of our social lives and built environments.

While we are now able to see evidence for ourselves, we all have conflicting ideas of what bit to attend to, and what it means. The camera may not lie, but that is because it does not speak at all. As we become more fixated on some ultimate gold standard of objective truth, which exceeds the words of mere journalists or experts, so the number of interpretations applied to the evidence multiplies. As our faith in the idea of undeniable proof deepens, so our frustration with competing framings and official accounts rises. All too often, the charge of 'bias' means 'that's not my perspective'. Our screen-based interactions with many institutions have become fuelled by anger that our experiences are not being better recognised, along with a new pleasure at being able to complain about it. As the writer and programmer Paul

Ford wrote, back in 2011, 'the fundamental question of the web' is: 'Why wasn't I consulted?'[14]

Digital populism

What we are witnessing is a collision between two conflicting ideals of truth: one that depends on trusted intermediaries (journalists and experts), and another that promises the illusion of direct access to reality itself. This has echoes of the populist challenge to liberal democracy, which pits direct expressions of the popular will against parliaments and judges, undermining the very possibility of compromise. The Brexit crisis exemplifies this as well as anything. Liberals and Remainers adhere to the long-standing constitutional convention that the public speaks via the institutions of general elections and Parliament. Adamant Brexiteers believe that the people spoke for themselves in June 2016, and have been thwarted ever since by MPs and civil servants. It is this latter logic that paints suspending Parliament as an act of democracy.

This is the tension that many populist leaders exploit. Officials and elected politicians are painted as cynically self-interested, while the 'will of the people' is both pure and obvious. Attacks on the mainstream media follow an identical script: the individuals professionally tasked with informing the public, in this case journalists, are biased and fake. It is widely noted that leaders such as Donald Trump, Jair Bolsonaro and Matteo Salvini are enthusiastic users of Twitter, and Boris Johnson has recently begun to use Facebook Live to speak directly to 'the people' from Downing Street. Whether it be parliaments or broadcasters, the analogue intermediaries of the public sphere are discredited and circumvented.

What can professional editors and journalists do in response? One option is to shout even louder about their commitment to 'truth', as some American newspapers have profitably done in the face of Trump. But this escalates cultural conflict, and fails to account for how the media and informational landscape has changed in the past twenty years.

What if, instead, we accepted the claim that all reports about the world are simply framings of one kind or another, which cannot but involve political and moral ideas about what counts as important? After all, reality becomes incoherent and overwhelming unless it is simplified and narrated in some way or other. And what if we accepted that journalists, editors and public figures will inevitably let cultural and personal biases slip from time to time? A shrug is often the more appropriate response than a howl. If we abandoned the search for some pure and unbiased truth, where might our critical energies be directed instead?

If we recognise that reporting is always a political act (at least in the sense that it asserts the importance of one story rather than another), then the key question is not whether it is biased, but whether it is independent of financial or political influence. The problem becomes a quasi-constitutional one, of what processes, networks and money determine how data gets turned into news, and how power gets distributed. On this front, the British media is looking worse and worse with every year that passes. The relationship between the government and the press has been getting tighter since the

1980s. This is partly thanks to the overweening power of Rupert Murdoch, and the image management that developed in response. Spin doctors such as Alastair Campbell, Andy Coulson, Tom Baldwin, Robbie Gibb and Seumas Milne typically moved from the media into party politics, weakening the division between the two.

Then there are those individuals who shift backwards and forwards between senior political positions and the BBC, such as Gibb, Rona Fairhead and James Purnell. The press has taken a very bad turn over recent years, with ex-chancellor George Osborne becoming editor of the *Evening Standard*, then the extraordinary recent behaviour of the *Daily Telegraph*, which seeks to present whatever story or gloss is most supportive of their former star columnist in 10 Downing Street, and rubbishes his opponents.

Since the financial crisis of 2008, there have been regular complaints about the revolving door between the financial sector and governmental institutions around the world, most importantly the White House. There has been far less criticism of the similar door that links the media and politics. The exception to this comes from populist leaders, who routinely denounce all 'mainstream' democratic and media institutions as a single liberal elite that acts against the will of the people. One of the reasons they are able to do this is because there is a grain of truth in what they say.

The financial obstacles confronting critical, independent, investigative media are significant. If the Johnson administration takes a more sharply populist turn, the political obstacles could increase, too – Channel 4 is frequently held up as an enemy of Brexit, for example. But let us be clear that an independent, professional media is what we need to defend at the present moment, and abandon the misleading and destructive idea that – thanks to a combination of ubiquitous data capture and personal passions – the truth can be grasped directly, without anyone needing to report it.

Mutations of leadership

Where to start with the sheer strangeness, let alone the danger, of the current situation in British politics? One place would be with the three characters at the centre of events. As the tectonic plates of the British State rumble ominously, take a moment to register quite how strange it is that the headlines should be dominated by the figures of Boris Johnson, Jeremy Corbyn and Dominic Cummings. Absent the idiosyncrasies of these men, and how they determine their interactions, the present crisis would be playing out in a different way entirely.

The central fact of Johnson's political career is that he has harboured a desire for high office since he was a child (we are told), but had scant interest in what he might do with it should he get it. David Cameron explained that he wanted to be prime minister 'because I think I'd be good at it', but this is something Johnson has never maintained about himself. The evidence to the contrary is already accumulating rapidly. And yet, there he sits, unelected but in office, a wish fulfilled.

Johnson has no ideology and no philosophy. It isn't even clear he has ambition, beyond making a point of having got where he's got. His residence in 10 Downing Street

represents a personal triumph, which he will want to prolong as long as possible, by whatever means possible. It is a
reflection on Britain's constitution that it is being pushed to
its limit by a man who has no vision of the nation beyond
his own pre-eminence in it. The media spent the Conservative leadership election posing questions about Johnson's
'character', yet the graver and more complicated question
is how the Tory party and the Westminster village allowed
themselves to become vehicles for one man's personal fantasy. Johnson has the single political advantage of being
well known by the public, but he is scarcely liked, let alone
admired. The reality is that his main qualification for office
is that he wants it more than anyone else. Brought low by
decades of division and ideological torpor, Conservative
MPs seemed unable to imagine any better credential.

Rarely can the term Her Majesty's Opposition have reso-
nated as strongly as when Johnson and Corbyn faced each
other across the dispatch box in the House of Commons.
The differences between these men go well beyond policy
or ideology; they reach into more basic questions of human
psychology and what Max Weber called the 'vocation' of
politics. Corbyn, of course, never wanted to lead anything,
let alone the country. It wasn't until the age of sixty-six,
when it was 'his turn' to stand as the left-wing candidate
in a Labour leadership election, that he was thrust into the
position of prospective prime minister.

The result, now that Johnson is in Downing Street, is
a quite extraordinary polarity. We have one leader who
has spent his entire life imagining himself standing on the
steps of Number 10 (it was noted that, as he entered for

the first time as prime minister, he was waving with one hand, while the other rested in his suit pocket, thumb protruding – an exact replica of a favourite Churchill pose), and another leader who was past retirement age before the daunting prospect even occurred to him. We have one man whose entire career has been built on passionate ethical commitments, most notably as an anti-war campaigner and advocate of Palestinian rights, and another who seems devoid of a single enduring belief.

Corbyn, to be sure, has demonstrated more political acumen, and above all more tenacity, than many would have predicted in the summer of 2015. He has also picked up political skills that Johnson was supposed to have learned at Eton and Oxford, but plainly didn't. Johnson's supporters in the House of Commons have had many disappointing reality checks over the course of his short premiership, but none can have been more distressing than the sight of their leader flailing around at Prime Minister's Questions, as Corbyn took him to pieces. What, after all, is the point of Johnson, if he can't dismiss his opponents with a clever turn of phrase? What, indeed, is the point of the Oxford Union, if one of its most celebrated presidents can't win a debate against an Islington hippy? The proroguing of Parliament couldn't come soon enough for Johnson.

Yet no matter how skilfully Corbyn plays his hand in the short term, it's his CV and his freakish pathway to the leadership that will always count more heavily. And this is integral to the political impasse created by Brexit. If Corbyn were a 'normal' leader, who had risen to the leadership by a typical route, there would be a simple way out of this crisis: a vote of no confidence would be called, and the leader of the opposition would be invited to form a coalition government. Given the impressive levels of cooperation across the 'rebel alliance' of Labour, Liberal Democrats, SNP and Tory rebels, the new prime minister would have every chance of working out a Brexit policy that could get through the House of Commons. But the prospect of a Corbyn government has become an exceptional factor in all of this: it's the one thing that hardcore Leavers see as worse than remaining, and the one thing hardcore Remainers see as worse than leaving.

What is it about Corbyn that puts him beyond the pale? There are several reasons for the widespread animosity towards him, foremost among them the sustained problem of antisemitism that has dogged the party under his leadership. But it's not clear that this alone renders his premiership unthinkable. Conservative newspapers and columnists refer to his 'Marxism' as a shorthand way of painting him as dangerous. But this has always been something of a red herring. Unlike John McDonnell (who cut his teeth as chair of finance at the radical GLC in the early 1980s), Corbyn has shown little interest in economic policy during his career, dedicating far more energy to opposing imperialism abroad than economics at home. In any case, recent noises from the City suggest that even the banks are now far better disposed towards a Corbyn government (which would at the very least ensure a customs union with Europe) than a no-deal Johnson administration.

There is a more fundamental reason why, as far as many Westminster insiders and much of the public are concerned,

Corbyn cannot become prime minister, and it has nothing to do with putting workers on company boards: he is ideologically opposed to the use of violence. This is why questions surrounding national security and nuclear war will always dog him, and why, when push comes to shove, even many centrists would prefer the chaos of no deal, overseen by a mendacious man-child, to Prime Minister Corbyn. At least that mendacious man-child will be willing to use the full range of tools at the state's disposal.

Weber saw modern political leadership as a balancing act between commitment to ultimate goals, and responsibility for the potentially devastating tools that the state uses to pursue them. Too much of the former ('an ethic of ultimate ends') and you have delusional zealotry, oblivious to the harm that is done in the service of idealism. Too much of the latter, and you have machine politics, where energy is focused on questions of efficiency and delivery. But whatever the circumstances, the ultimate tool of the state is always violence, and a 'responsible' politician is one who keeps this brute truth in mind.

By Weber's definition it isn't clear that a pacifist can ever be a politician, let alone a national leader. Or rather, it isn't possible to remain a pacifist once you have taken charge of a modern state. You either assume 'responsibility' for the violent operation you are leading, or continue reciting your dogma of 'ultimate ends' while turning your back on the consequences. It's well known that on the day a new prime minister takes office their duties include writing a letter to nuclear submarine commanders, giving them instructions on what action to take in the event that Britain has been wiped out in a nuclear attack. There is a deathly substrate to the state and its highest offices that seems almost ontologically incompatible with Jeremy Corbyn's image of himself. This is the reason his followers adore him, and the reason too that the (far larger) ranks of sceptics will never accept him as part of a compromise.

Weber had Johnson's number. He warned against the politician whose 'vanity' turns the pursuit of power into a 'purely personal self-intoxication', who strives 'for the glamorous semblance of power, rather than for actual power'. And yet, because 'striving for power is one of the driving forces of all politics, there is no more harmful distortion of political force than the parvenu-like braggart with power, and the vain self-reflection in the feeling of power'.[15] Johnson may be in it for the posh banquets and Churchillian photos, but the consequences are far, far weightier. It is because he is so uninterested in consequences that he has delegated so much power to his chief strategist.

Dominic Cummings has become an object of fascination thanks to his brazen disregard for rules and his dabbling in the exotic arts of rationalist theorising. His dense and rambling blogposts, among them the interminable 'Some thoughts on education and political priorities', are now the site of an archaeological dig for anyone seeking to divine the underlying logic of Johnson's apparently chaotic administration. There is a guilty frisson in the idea of a lawless nihilist pulling all the strings, but to grasp the danger Cummings poses, one has to start by recognising how ordinary his core assumptions are. One thing that is certain and consistent in the Cummings outlook is that MPs are a pompous waste of space, and civil servants are a cartel of self-interested cowards, whose main function is thwarting policy. These views are thought appalling in Westminster and Whitehall for obvious reasons, but in pubs up and down the country, they are almost an orthodoxy.

What is unusual is not that Cummings should hold these views, but that he has held them while pursuing a career in Whitehall. His condemnation of a stagnant public sector is seen as common sense in much of the business world, especially the world of e-government contractors and public sector outsourcing, whose shtick rests on the idea that government is crap at doing stuff. Tony Blair's obsession with 'public service modernisation', built on the creed that 'what matters is what works', provided an adjacent justification for outsourcing and endless managerial reforms: they would, it was said, inject more dynamism, efficiency and 'leadership' into the public sector. Cummings is in some ways the logical conclusion of this relentless modernising mentality, in which the state is always deficient in comparison to business.

Except, of course, that it isn't just public services he is trying to shake up. His antipathy to stasis now seems to apply to virtually any convention or institution of British public life. The Conservative Party, the House of Commons, the 'purdah' rules (which seek to prevent the civil service being used for political ends during an election campaign), data protection, normal relations with the media, the Electoral Commission, and possibly the rule of law itself, are all viewed as obstacles to circumvent in pursuit of some goal. His boss's goal is clear: to remain in Downing Street.

What Cummings wants, other than the further humiliation of British elites, is less clear. For the time being, though, Johnson's possession of an attack dog, willing to tear away at the basic conditions of liberal democracy, looks like an electoral asset, now that a sizeable proportion of the electorate has decided that democracy is a sham.

So: a prime minister who is in office mainly because he so badly wants to be; a leader of the opposition who is both loved and loathed for being so unlike a political leader; and a government strategist who despises government. It is as if a conventional modern politician had been broken in three: add Johnson's personal ambition to Corbyn's piety, and combine them with Cummings's technocratic zeal, and you might get someone a bit like Blair – the very model of the 'responsible' politician Weber had in mind, and the last thing most voters want right now. We are living with the consequences of a prolonged and deepening anti-politics.

Deference to our sometime political superiors has been in decline for more than half a century. The sense of alarm when (apparently on Cummings's instruction) twenty-one Conservative MPs were purged from the party for voting in favour of an extension to Article 50 was partly a reflection of the ruthlessness of that action, but also an expression of sentimental feeling for the old duffers being punished. In their crumpled suits and schoolboy ties they seemed so harmless! When the grandson of Winston Churchill (Sir Nicholas Soames) and the great-great-grandson of Lord Salisbury (Richard Benyon) are being booted out, it would seem that the age of cap-doffing is well and truly over. But Cummings was merely accelerating a trend.

How does liberal democracy work, once tradition, class and culture no longer identify appropriate governors? The success of neoliberalism, which emerged as a new policy paradigm in the late 1970s, derived as much from its solution to this problem as from its economic outcomes, which have always been questionable. At the heart of neoliberal philosophy was the idea that markets are smarter than governments because they factor in millions of ordinary opinions and expectations, whereas governments rely on a coterie of over-confident experts and planners. Markets aren't just efficient, but democratic. They give everyone a say.

Privatisation, deregulation, PFI and other pro-market reforms worked with the grain of a public that was increasingly sceptical of public authorities and politics in general. Blair's gambit was that only by keeping pace with the expectations of an increasingly consumerist culture could public services retain credibility and support. This may have been true in the medium term, but eventually it leaves the public sector without any justification or cultural identity of its own. It is a state-led strategy for hollowing out and talking down public service (as distinct from business), one that was followed even as New Labour was pouring unprecedented sums of money into public services.

Meanwhile, Parliament and parties did less and less. Party membership and electoral turn-outs declined. It isn't irrelevant that the period in which publics across the world slowly deserted their political institutions was also one of economic stability and policy consensus. Politics no longer seemed to provide answers to the questions that mattered, either to citizens or to policymakers. This was the crucible of the Cummings worldview.

It's now clear that the financial crisis of 2008, and the years of austerity that followed, had the effect of discrediting neoliberal dogmas about the market, but – contrary to the initial hopes of the left – without restoring confidence in government or democracy. A diffuse mood of anti-elitism, targeted at business, media, politics and government, has created a residual sense that institutions have been rigged by insiders. Johnson, Corbyn and Cummings, each in his own way, harness and express this populist instinct. Each is jostling to be the beneficiary of institutional decay.

The danger for Labour, which is also the danger for liberal democracy, is that the EU referendum has become viewed by many Leavers (and their sympathisers in the media) as the only uncorrupted political institution left. The Johnson-Cummings script is a beautifully simple one: 'the people' spoke in June 2016, but the politicians weren't prepared to listen. The more enemies Johnson makes in Westminster, Whitehall and the courts, the more he demonstrates his fidelity to the one true act of democracy. The more often he is defeated – even to the point of humiliation – the more he proves his mettle to the 17.4 million who have been denied what they were promised. Corbyn's defence of Parliament and the rule of law makes him look statesmanlike, but it also exposes him to the attack lines that will be deployed once the Cummings electoral machine kicks into gear in the autumn.

But nailing Corbyn as part of 'the elite' is scarcely going to wash. He can't be the face of Parliament *and* a threat to national security. He can't be a liberal Remainer *and* an insurrectionary Marxist. As Theresa May found in June 2017, Corbyn is a much trickier political opponent than he often appears to be, and he remains the most plausible alternative to another Johnson-Cummings government. Before very long, we will be witnessing an electoral showdown between the man who would do anything to appear 'prime ministerial', and the one who has often appeared anything but. These are strange and unpredictable forms of authority; only a fool would claim to know which way it will go.

The Party of Resentment

What does the Conservative Party stand for in 2019? If you survey the central tenets of Tory ideology from the past fifty years, it is hard to find a single one that is still intact. The party of business is hell-bent on undermining access to an export market of half a billion people. The party of law and order is now raging against the judiciary – with senior Tories being regularly asked whether their government intends to obey the law. The party of 'family values' – 'back to basics', as John Major put it – has now fallen for the charms of a famous philanderer, who reportedly doesn't know how many children he has. The party of the establishment is provoking a constitutional crisis, angering the Queen and expelling some of its most distinguished MPs from its benches.

So perhaps the more pertinent question is whether there is anything the Conservative Party *won't* stand for. But the answer to that isn't much clearer either: the Johnson-Cummings strategy depends on cultivating the sense that they will say or do anything to achieve their ends; their only principle is a refusal to rule anything out. And to the extent that they face any constraints, these are not coming from inside the Conservative Party.

Surviving Tory moderates kid themselves that the problem is all with Boris Johnson's chief adviser, Dominic Cummings, as if they hadn't fallen into line behind a man famed for dishonesty and recklessness. They kid themselves that the party is still theirs, as if it hadn't swelled with Brexit fanatics with no interest in governing. The fact that Amber Rudd resigned (in September 2019) simultaneously from the cabinet *and* the Conservative whip clarified the stakes: the current toxicity belongs to the party, not any individual strategist or leader.

For a party that had been losing its political and philosophical moorings for many years, Brexit has become a substitute for ideology – something more potent and emotional than just a vision for a good society or a policy manifesto. For Conservative Party members and many MPs, Brexit is almost theological: it is a crusade requiring sacrifice and suffering. It is not possible that the reality of Brexit will ever live up to the divine version, while parliamentary democracy now appears hopelessly compromised in comparison with the pure 'will of the people' that the 2016 referendum is believed to have revealed.

This fanaticism is being escalated and exploited by men without any apparent ideology of their own, or even any particular faith in Brexit. On the actual question posed by the referendum, Boris Johnson was famously ambivalent. And after writing tens of thousands of words about British

politics on his own blog, it's still not clear how Cummings
really thinks society should look, or if he even identifies
as a 'conservative'. These men are opportunists, for whom
nationalist fervour and chaos provide an opening to seize
power. And a party in the grip of collective mania is more
vulnerable to such machinations than one with a coherent
ideology.

To pinpoint the origins of this ideological decline, one
has to look back much further than the referendum. The
identity and purpose of the Conservative Party has been
slowly unravelling for three decades. The year of the 'big
bang' was 1986, when the City of London was dramatically
deregulated, disrupting the old-boy networks of Britain's
business classes with the shock of a new, aggressive style of
international finance. The subsequent explosion of wealth
opened up a cultural and financial schism between London
and England – sowing seeds of resentment in the shires that
would blossom in 2016.

But 1986 was also the high point of Tory Europeanism,
the year of the Single European Act, which set Europe on
the path to a single market, and was driven and crafted by
Margaret Thatcher and her allies. Before this point, the crusade for 'free markets' was an ideological rallying cry for
the New Right backers of Ronald Reagan and Thatcher –
a soaring ambition that could only be brought to fruition
by brave leaders in their mould. Now it would become a
technocratic and regulatory project, overseen by bureau-
crats and lawyers. With the demise of state socialism three
years later, capitalism no longer needed the Conservative
Party. And business soon found a better friend in New

Labour – which offered state-of-the-art regulation and a culture of innovation – than it has found before or since.

Over those thirty years, there was one force in Britain's public life that never gave up on the Tories: the press. All those resentments that took the place of Conservative ideology – the loathing of multiculturalism, Brussels, Blairism, immigration, and the vast riches being made in London – were given a safe space in the pages of the *Daily Mail*, the *Daily Express* and the *Daily Telegraph*. With their constant attacks on all symptoms of liberal globalisation, these papers provided the incubator for the rage currently sweeping British politics, during the long years when national borders and rural England were out of political fashion.

With one of those newspapers' favourite sons ensconced in Number 10, the boundary between the opinion pages and Westminster has dissolved. The resentments that had brewed for decades – towards 'political correctness' and the milieu of metropolitan graduates – now flood public life, with the arrival of a prime minister who speaks his mind as recklessly at the dispatch box as he once did on the page. What these forces of reaction stand for is not 'free markets' or 'private enterprise', but the sort of back-scratching, long-lunching privileges that once made the establishment tick.

The collapsing division between the Conservative Party and the conservative press has produced an optical illusion in which the concerns of the party are constantly mistaken for those of the country. One of the curiosities of David Cameron's recent round of memoir-promoting interviews was his complete inability to distinguish between 'Europe' as a problem facing the nation (where fewer than 10 per cent of the public deemed it to be an important issue, right up to 2016), and Europe as a problem ripping through the Tory party.

No explanation of Brexit – and hence of the worst political crisis in living memory – can escape the truth that it was born, nurtured and released into society from the Conservative backbenches. The party has done for British democracy what derivatives did to the financial sector – and it has so far survived the carnage it produced. Instead, blame for the chaos has been sprayed in all directions: on to Europeans, Labour, Remainers and 'the elites', thanks to the symbiotic relationship between party and press.

Johnson could win a workable majority in the next few months. And yet there's a marked absence of triumphalism in the party. The current poll lead feels precarious; 59 per cent of Tory members have already voted for the Brexit Party once (in the European Parliament elections), and many could well do so in future. The Conservatives are now to the Brexit Party what cocaine is to crack: more acceptable in polite company, but ultimately made of the same stuff. Rage and resentment are powerful political forces, but dangerously unpredictable. Unlike a newspaper columnist, a prime minister takes far more flak than he dishes out, and Johnson now appears harried and uncomfortable. Lacking any positive vision of the economy or society, he and Cummings are entirely reliant on channelling resentment towards various foes, from Supreme Court justices to Jeremy Corbyn. The newspapers will do their bit by escalating the attacks. But these nemeses cannot soak up all that anger indefinitely. The forces behind Brexit will need new scapegoats soon – and Johnson, Cummings and the Conservative Party could be next in line.

The Berlusconification of Britain

If this general election campaign has a distinctive mood, it is a mix of bewilderment, outrage and exhaustion. The public sphere has been engulfed by a war of attrition in which every poll number, media statement or policy announcement must be treated with suspicion. What is it concealing? Who paid for it? What is it distracting us from? The rules of engagement seem alien and unstable. Apart from the trolls-for-hire running the Conservative Party digital media strategy, it's hard to imagine that anyone is enjoying this. Political campaigns have always been an exercise in attention-seeking and the sabotaging of opponents' messaging, deploying classic military tactics of surprise and deception in the process, but this has now escalated to a point where meaningful argument has become all but impossible. Stand back for a moment, and a bigger question dawns: is this what the end of liberalism feels like?

If 2016 was the year that liberals discovered the vulnerability of 'fact-based' political campaigning, 2019 feels more like a wholesale institutional crisis. Liberal democracy depends on public confidence that certain rules and structures are beyond political influence or manipulation, basic journalistic norms of reporting included. Even if the media has never been perfectly neutral or independent, they have traditionally occupied a separate – if sometimes overlapping – sphere to the political parties and leaders they report on. And so, with considerable imperfections, the media once provided a stage for the contest between rival parties. Now this distinction – between the frame around politics and its contents – appears to have dissolved. Never before have the media been so internal to the arguments that have played out over the course of an election campaign. It seems that every televised debate, interview (or avoidance thereof) and journalist's tweet sets off a fresh conflict of attack and counter-attack, dragging supposedly impartial bodies such as the BBC into the theatre of informational war.

The immediate catalyst for our current chaos lies in the reckless strand of conservatism that now dominates the Tory party, thanks to the crisis of Brexit and the opportunism of Boris Johnson. The mentality of this New Right is one that is hostile to the very idea of 'neutral' or 'independent' institutions as checks on power; they are viewed as sclerotic and self-interested. Much has been written about the philosophy of Dominic Cummings in this respect, but it was Michael Gove who elevated Cummings in the first place – and who is now sowing confusion and disinformation in the media as enthusiastically as anyone. The entire Conservative election platform hangs on the idea that Parliament and Whitehall are betraying 'the people' – that is, they are pursuing their own political agenda. In this view, everyone has already picked a side – and if you refuse to state your choice, you are marked as left-wing, probably a Remainer, and potentially disloyal to Britain.

The once separate domains marked 'politics' and 'media' have collapsed into each other. It is not incidental that the politicians leading the charge against fair reporting – Johnson and Gove – are both former journalists. They dwell in a space *between* politics and news, where everything becomes about performing for the camera, manipulating the frame and controlling the audience experience. Britain is used to having the majority of newspapers pitted against the Labour Party, and expects every Labour leader to come under disproportionate attack. But the combination of Brexit and Johnson has produced something altogether new: a sense that Downing Street is now a media agency, and Fleet Street a political one.

One of the cornerstones of liberal politics, dating back to the Enlightenment, is the idea of a 'separation of powers'. This typically refers to the tripartite system of government, separating executive, legislature and judiciary, on which the US constitution was built. But liberalism depends on other varieties of separation, or at least the appearance of them. It assumes, for instance, that 'the economy' is relatively separate from 'the state'. To most liberals, even the concentration of power in specific institutions – such as large corporations – is acceptable so long as that power is contested by rivals. What is fatal for liberalism, however, is the semblance of a single, undivided power bloc, or the emergence of one centre of power that dominates all others.

Without some distinction between rival centres of power, public decision-making cannot possibly be described as 'fair' or 'independent'. Only if judges retain their distance from parliamentary politics, for example, can their judgements be perceived as disinterested. By the same token, the BBC can perform its role in providing an 'impartial' account of political events only if its distance from party politics is defended and respected. But a key tactic of the new conservatism is to mock the very idea of 'fairness', toying with it to the point where it becomes merely cosmetic – as when the Conservative Twitter account was briefly rebranded as factcheckUK.[16]

Johnson, Gove and Cummings are exploiting institutional decay, but they didn't initiate it. Various ideological and technological forces have been undermining the conditions of liberal pluralism for some years. During the 1990s, a new orthodoxy developed among political scientists and sociologists that power now resided in networks, not institutions; for individuals, 'networking' became a crucial career skill. In place of professionalism (focused on a single domain of practice), a new ethos emerged to celebrate flexibility and self-reinvention – the ability to leap from job to job and sector to sector as the market demands.

The simultaneous rise of the internet broke down the vertical divisions – slowly at first, and then all at once – between different genres of culture and communication. Where once there were newspapers, broadcasts, magazines, drama and light entertainment, now there are platforms where a torrent of undifferentiated 'content' spills around. The political troll and the fake-news merchant exploit a simple truth – that it's no longer possible to keep spaces marked 'satire' and 'news' away from each other. This new information ecosystem has given rise to a new type of public figure, who does not belong in any one of the old analogue domains, being at once an actor, a comedian, a politician and a media personality. Look no further than our prime minister.

Elites have always had means of congregating, be they

Oxford University clubs or exclusive schools. But in the past these served as institutional escalators, providing rapid access to the heights of an establishment subdivided by professional specialism. In today's power elite, figures such as George Osborne don't expect to have to choose between a career in politics, finance or the media, but flit between them. We are witnessing a kind of 'Berlusconification' of public life, where the divisions between politics, media and business lose all credibility. Legitimacy crises of this sort are disastrous for public trust – but they offer tantalising opportunities to a handful of individuals willing to take advantage.

Brexit isn't the cause of this slow collapse, so much as its most disruptive consequence. But it is also an accelerator. Brexit is what you believe in once you've come to see public life as a game played by insiders. And the reason you come to that conclusion is partly because it contains some truth. The more dubious government, party politics and the media appear, the more seductive Brexit grows, and the deeper Johnson's support becomes. Downing Street understands this, which is why it is determined to make public life look as dubious as possible.

The Johnson Victory

After a chaotic and surreal campaign, there was a comforting familiarity about the rituals of election night. Tories will rehearse their favourite fairy-tale – that the 'party of Thatcher' has finally rediscovered its 1980s mojo – while Labour retreats to its own comfort zone of bitter internal feuding. But amid all this drama, there is a danger that we might forget how deeply abnormal the Conservative election campaign has been, and how frighteningly unfamiliar the impending government could be.

The winning campaign strategy was simple: to make this the second referendum, to make it as exhausting as possible, and to make sure Labour's offer of yet another referendum looked more exhausting still. The Tories' blank policy agenda – beyond passing the existing Brexit deal in January – was aimed directly at a group of voters who don't trust politicians, don't believe government can help them, and are done with listening to 'liberal elites' bickering over the precise number of hospitals the Tories will or won't build. For today's Conservatives, the collapse of trust in institutions isn't a problem – it's an opportunity. 'Get Brexit Done', like Donald Trump's 'build a wall', was not a policy pledge so much as a mantra to identify with, for those who think the establishment is a stitch-up.

Two other ingredients were necessary. First, a right-wing 'big tent' needed constructing, one that spreads all the way from Matt Hancock in the centre-right out to Tommy Robinson on the far right. Johnson repeatedly did just enough to communicate to former Brexit Party voters that he was on their side. For the desperate men and women (but mostly men) living in the abandoned economic regions of the Midlands and the North, for whom only a Trump figure would be enough to draw them to the polls, Johnson performed that role adequately. For well-off elderly voters, who had been seduced by Faragist visions of national identity, Johnson's dog-whistles hit home. Study his 'apologies' for past Islamophobic comments, and you'll notice that they're never apologies at all – they are affirmations of his right to say 'what everyone is thinking'.

Second, Johnson's media profile and contacts were leveraged to the hilt. By the end of the campaign, he was performing a kind of Jeremy Clarkson role – obliterating any democratic dialogue or interrogation by dressing up as a milkman or driving a forklift truck. 'Boris' began life as a construct of the *Daily Telegraph* and *Have I Got News For You*, but now exists as a genre of social media 'content'. Unlike in the heyday of broadcast and print media, propaganda now has to be lively and engaging in order to work. And so the election was not won by an ordinary political party, with policies, members and ideology. It was won by a single-issue new-media start-up – you might call it Vote Boris – fronted by a TV star, which will now unveil a largely unknown policy agenda.

The 2016 referendum result and the 'Boris' phenomenon have created a Trojan Horse, within which lurks who knows what. But the chances of it offering anything transformative to the former Labour voters of Blyth Valley or Bolsover, beyond the occasional culture-war titbit, are minimal. One thing we do know is that the Vote Boris campaign was funded by hedge funds and wealthy British entrepreneurs – just as they donated heavily to Vote Leave. But who knows what they get in return? It also seems safe to assume, on the evidence of Johnson's first few months in office, that his administration will be hostile to many basic norms of the constitution and the liberal public sphere. Meanwhile, a triumphant Dominic Cummings will have his eye on a drastic transformation of Whitehall and regulators, inspired by exotic forms of rationalism, game theory and the libertarian right.

If the new Johnson government sustains its unprecedented relationship with the media of the past six weeks – threatening public service broadcasters, excluding the *Daily Mirror* from its campaign bus, seamless coordination with the conservative press, using 'Boris' to distract from every unwelcome news item – then it will be virtually impossible for it to be held to account for what it does. And having already rebranded itself as the 'people's government', there is no reason to expect it will embrace normal democratic scrutiny or opposition.

A combination of Brexit, decades of neglect and political alienation in Labour's heartlands, the new digital media ecology, and hints of frightening illiberalism could conspire to produce a form of democracy that looks more like Hungary or even Russia than the checks-and-balances system of liberal ideals. It's not that democracy will end, but that it will be reduced to a set of spectacles that the government is ultimately in command of, which everyone realises are 'fake' but that are sufficiently funny or soothing as to be tolerated.

This may sound paranoid, but it is merely an extrapolation from the trends that are already in full sway. Just like Trump, Johnson's capacity to make headlines and change the subject means we can quickly forget how much damage he has already done, in less than six months – instead we are locked in a perpetual present, squabbling over the details of what he's doing right now. It's important to keep track. Challenging this juggernaut will be a far larger and more complex project than anything Her Majesty's Opposition can do alone.

Afterword:
In the Wreckage of Liberalism

Within two months of the 2019 general election, Boris Johnson had delivered on the one substantial policy pledge of his triumphant electoral campaign: on 31 January 2020, Britain exited the European Union. This produced the unusual and uneasy state of affairs whereby a new prime minister with a sizeable majority had close to five years of power ahead of him, with precious little public knowledge of what he intended to use it for. Considerable uncertainty hovered around Johnson's domestic agenda and his own political vision, which appeared to change depending on what was the easiest or most entertaining line to take from one moment to the next. In the event, Johnson enjoyed the shortest of honeymoons before an even bigger crisis than Brexit appeared in March 2020. Things were about to get a lot less normal.

Once the scale and implications of the COVID-19 pandemic had become clear, the tone of the Johnson leadership became dramatically different. The bluster, recklessness, humour and optimism which his supporters adored were suddenly absent. At the very historical juncture when Britain had witnessed a popular revenge against unelected technocrats and liberal institutions, an emergency arrived that placed huge public demands on scientists and administrators, throwing statistics into the media spotlight for weeks on end. Following months in which Johnson and his supporters had turned politics into a festival of flag-waving, trolling, rule-breaking and mendacity, there was now an urgent need to focus on verifiable facts and communicate as precisely as possible. Daily press conferences were established, at which Johnson or a cabinet colleague would stand flanked by scientific advisors.

As March turned into April, and Britain's death toll mounted, the era of 'fake news' and divisive cultural battles seemed to have receded into the distant past. In the depths of the crisis, with a full lockdown under way, some observers wondered whether a government of 'national unity' would have to be established. Johnson's populist targeting of independent institutions, such as the BBC, supreme court, Whitehall and universities, was put on hold. It appeared that, amidst the turmoil, liberal elites had won a reprieve.

But within little more than a month, the pendulum was swinging back again. Following the prime minister's hospitalisation with COVID-19, his cheerleaders in the press went into overdrive in celebrating his persona as a national hero. A new wave of national iconography began to swell, of flags, World War Two songs, royalty and appeals to collective sacrifice. The National Health Service was conscripted as part of this glorious national effort, evidence of a uniquely *British* spirit of resilience and optimism. Hiding behind all this rhetoric and symbolism was the worst mortality rate in Europe, concentrated among deprived inner city communities, especially ethnic minorities. The constant rhetorical emphasis on 'our NHS' disguised the fact that nearly half of deaths were occurring in care homes, outside of the government's official statistics, and to where elderly people were being rapidly transferred from hospitals, potentially bringing infections with them.

A crisis that initially appeared to have transcended cultural and political divides was soon being exploited to fend off criticism of Johnson's leadership. Stories emerged of particular journalists being barred from asking questions at press conferences. Matt Hancock, the health secretary, accused Labour MP and medic Rosena Allin-Khan of adopting the wrong 'tone', when she challenged the government's failure in testing for the virus.

Above all, Johnson's support from the conservative press became deafening, and the 'Boris' character was mobilised to hide the facts of vast and fatal policy failures. The stream of inconvenient statistics and research findings were spun and disguised wherever possible, with one official report on mortality rates being delayed to hide its findings on the disproportionate threat to ethnic minorities. At every turn, the expectation was that the government should be the recipient of national solidarity, while their opponents were simply sowing division and pessimism. The unwinding of the daily press conferences was initially justified on the eminently Trumpian grounds that they did not attract sufficient 'ratings'.

As Johnson and his government slowly recovered from the depths of April 2020, the attacks on independent institutions picked up all over again. The status of Johnson's strategist Dominic Cummings was cast into a whole new light, following the scandal that erupted from the discovery that he had repeatedly ignored the government's rules of lockdown. Not only was Cummings entirely unrepentant, but – in supporting him so slavishly – it became palpably obvious that Downing Street had no respect for erstwhile norms of public life. This may have been no surprise to anyone who had closely followed the Brexit campaign (led by Cummings) or the Johnson leadership, but in the context of such terrible national stress, it felt as if the entire country was being trolled by a joker figure.

As more and more policy failures came to light (with one former scientific advisor estimating that the delay in the March lockdown had led to twice as many deaths by June), the Johnson government renewed its efforts to initiate culture wars, as a shroud over the social and personal catastrophes that were unfolding. Conservative politicians launched into arguments over historic statues, war memorials, trans rights and criminal justice in an effort to change the topic and discredit their critics.

And yet by summer 2020, with public trust in government's handling of the crisis plummeting (especially in the honesty of their information), the scale of the social, economic and racial crises across British – and especially English – society was more than government propaganda could hide.[1] As Johnson and his band of Brexiteers set about attacking the institutions of the liberal establishment, they themselves had precious few alternative grounds for legitimacy, beyond the best efforts of a desperately struggling print media industry.

In the summer of 2020, the Black Lives Matter protests, and the accompanying reckoning of historic institutions and wealth, brought an extraordinary flowering of political expression and criticism. Surreally, in the context of an ongoing lockdown of much of the economy and public space, new protest movements filled the void, where previously there were the rigours and routines of everyday capitalist society. Amid the stress of the pandemic, there were glimpses of alternative futures – less beholden to tradition, work, consumption and long-distance travel. One survey showed that the vast majority of people did not want to return to 'normal' patterns of life, once the crisis had finally passed.[2] The key pillars of liberal capitalism were questionable and questioned like never before, not just in terms of their past (which could now be publicly explored in relation to colonialism and slavery), but in terms of their future, which seemed less certain than they had for decades. The breaking of normality also represents liberation.

Nevertheless, in spite of these crises, failures and fresh hopes, the power of the post-Brexit Conservative regime remains fearsome. Its vision had already been hinted at over the previous years, as mapped in this book: much tighter national borders, attacks on universities and other centres of international intellectualism, weakening of checks on executive power (such as the independent civil service and judiciary), and intimidation of public service media such as the BBC and Channel 4, all combined with an 'unleashing' of the rights of capital. The economic and cultural opportunity of the COVID-19 crisis, from the perspective of the self-described 'post-liberals' on the right, is to push Britain away from the cosmopolitanism and openness that had been a general tendency since the 1960s, back towards a society of fewer university graduates, lower levels of migration and greater economic nationalism.

This potentially coincides with a cybernetic fantasy (popular with Cummings and his former patron, Michael Gove) of data-led policy-making, which in practice means shifting decision-making into opaque centres of commercial analytics contractors. The industry that benefited the most from the pandemic was that of digital platform monopolies. In late April 2020, one fifth of the value of the American S&P 500 was in just five companies: Amazon, Facebook, Alphabet (which owns Google), Apple and Microsoft. No matter how markets and society would be revived, much of it would be channelled via these apparently indomitable private powers. In spite of the brief hiatus, when public expertise and policy competence experienced a resurgence of enthusiasm from the Johnson government, the longer term effect of the pandemic looks likely to be a hastening of the collapse of British liberalism.

These forces leave the left in a similar bind as the Brexit split had done over the previous four years, only now without the galvanising force of the Corbyn leadership of the Labour Party that connected Westminster to more radical forces on the left. In the face of conservative and nationalist attacks on the liberal establishment, many on the left feel ambivalent. The shortcomings and occlusions of government administration, technocratic policy-making, scientific positivism, constitutionalism, liberal economics and public service broadcasting have all been subjected to sustained critique, from a range of Marxist and non-Marxist positions.

And yet these remain potential checks on a form of executive power that seems intent on reinstating traditional cultural hierarchies, in alliance with particular business interests – the form of 'neo-illiberalism' that has already been identified in the United States, Hungary and Brazil.[3] History suggests that liberal institutions alone are not enough to prevent the rise of nationalism, and may often be complicit with it; but it also suggests that the worst varieties of right-wing regime begin by targeting independent agencies and individuals, who can be charged with disloyalty or allegiance to international networks. For these reasons, the collapse of liberalism in the present context is cause for grave political concern.

In truth, this ambivalence is as old as socialism itself. Ever since the French Revolution, the starting point of socialist critique and organisation is that liberal freedoms are necessary but not sufficient. Freedom in the political realm is a mere abstraction, unless it is matched by freedom in the economic realm. The left has highlighted the fact that the bourgeois public sphere only admits property-owners as equals; and yet it has also exploited the freedoms of the public sphere to advance its arguments and interests, and is hostile to political efforts to constrain such liberties. Critical theorists in the Frankfurt School tradition have often sought to walk this dialectical path, of harnessing the methodologies and intellectual freedoms of bourgeois society to challenge, unmask and weaken the power of liberal capitalism.

In the context of neoliberalism, and especially in the wake of September 11, the left has found itself defending the norms and institutions of liberalism, often with little acknowledgement from the liberal establishment itself. As neoliberal reforms have sought to elevate financial mechanisms and metrics above legal ones, the defence of rights and due process has frequently become an anti-capitalist one. See, for instance, how liberal norms around privacy are an essential tool of resistance to the mission creep of 'surveillance capital'.

And as neoconservatives have sought to elevate executive decisions above legal and judicial authority, it has frequently been those on the left who are found deploying liberal–legal arguments against the state. On issues such as deportations, legal aid, detention without trial and 'extraordinary rendition', it has repeatedly been the left (and not the neoliberal centre) that has done the job of defending the rule of law and judicial process. Whenever legislation has entered Parliament seeking to empower the executive at the expense of civil liberties, it has been socialists in the Labour Party that have voted against.

Liberal ideals, of constitutional process and the 'separation of powers', have played a fundamental role in legitimating and sustaining capitalism since the eighteenth century, which renders them suspicious in the eyes of the left. But two additional things are worth noting. Firstly, it's no longer clear that contemporary capitalism has need of a norm-based, legal model of the state, indeed platform capitalism prospers by defying it. Companies such as Facebook and Google thrive by attacking existing norms around ownership and privacy; code acquires the sovereignty once reserved for law. This is where the 'disruptors' of Silicon Valley find a common cause with those of the new conservative insurgency.

Moreover, there is much to gain from diverting liberal ideals (of restraint on executive power) towards democratic socialism, and against the overbearing power of contemporary capital. As the liberal–legal state is dismantled, it is not the left that will be the beneficiary, but new combinations of the nationalist right and monopoly capital. The task, as Katharina Pistor has argued, is to seize the legal tools that enshrine the rights of capital, and divert them to alternative forms of economic ownership and control.[4]

The Deleuzian 'control society', now perfected by the Wall Street–Silicon Valley alliance, is one that attacks all forms of institutional differentiation. It replaces separate spaces of 'enclosure' with a 'continuous network', where everything is constantly connected to everything else. Leisure, work, education, healthcare and intimacy all blend into one, producing an exhausted individual who lacks any downtime or breaks. This is what the circumstances of the COVID-19 pandemic have accelerated. Here too, resistance often takes an implicitly liberal form: it is precisely the right of people to have separate spheres of life (public/private, political/economic, work/leisure) that, in their occasional naivety, liberals have sought to defend. For Marx, the length of the working day was the frontline of the battle between capital and labour.

Today it is the very possibility of a temporally differentiated life, and an institutionally differentiated society, that is at stake. This is why occupations and picket lines are both disruptive and constructive, seeing as they gesture towards the possibility of life lived in multiple modes, in multiple times and places. The recent collapse of 'work', 'home' and 'family' into a single confined space, deprived of a public, was provoked by the coronavirus, but there are numerous political and economic forces which seek to exploit and prolong it. To date, it has been women whose freedom has been most curtailed by this enforced domesticity.

Neoliberalism has grown increasingly illiberal since 2008, producing new mutations of nationalism and deregulation.[5] The main beneficiaries of this are the crony capitalists and political insiders who leach off the patrimonial state.[6] These include the financial and digital 'innovators', who are looking for regulations and legal oversight to be weakened or tweaked to suit their business interests, and who find plenty of supporters in the post-liberal state.

The politically fatal dimension of neoliberalism, since its intellectual inception in the 1930s, has been its refusal to distinguish between a 'political' and an 'economic' realm. Government becomes a branch of business; business becomes a mode of governance. Who cares what's public and what's private? But as liberal institutions gradually decay, this eventually results in a situation of rampant clientelism, in which centres of power and of money collapse into a single undifferentiated elite. This is an outcome that would work equally well for Boris Johnson, the City of London and Silicon Valley, and would be applauded by Rupert Murdoch's papers and broadcasters all the way.

The graver threat is of fascism, which seeks to abolish *both* the economic rights won by socialists, *and* the legal–constitutional ones established by liberals. The optimistic Marxist view of history, whereby each stage of economic development contains the seeds of its own destruction and superior replacement, runs into a violent obstacle where fascists are intent on stripping capitalism of all remnants of political modernity. The enemies of contemporary fascism are well known: socialists, feminists, critical theorists, plus of course the ethnic and cultural groups perceived to be controlling the global economy and 'replacing' white majorities. In wedding capitalism to metaphysical political visions of antiquity – of fatherhood, heroic violence, a bloodline and so on – the fascist takes aim indiscriminately at *all* emancipatory modern programmes. The question, then, is whether such programmes can forge alliances in time to resist.

If what's left of the liberal centre does not find a way of identifying common ground with the left, it will be welcomed in by the nationalist right. This is well underway in many democracies around the world. It seems too often that, while the left is willing to defend key liberal planks of political modernity such as human rights and attention to facts, this is not reciprocated with support for economic democracy and wholesale redistribution of wealth and income. The crisis ushered in by coronavirus has accelerated the need to find this common ground between the defenders of institutional norms and those who agitate for economic justice. Long-standing liberal–socialist ideals, such as universal basic income, have acquired unprecedented plausibility in the context of the global pandemic. If this moment is to be seized by something other than nationalism or a type of privatised platform technocracy, a coalition of legal and economic rebuilders will be needed.

Acknowledgements

The pieces in this book were originally published in the *Guardian*, the *London Review of Books*, the *New York Times*, openDemocracy and the blog of the Political Economy Research Centre. I'm very grateful to the various editors who commissioned the essays and played a vital role in honing them: Rosemary Bechler, Paul Myerscough and his colleagues at the *LRB*, Jonathan Shainin, Max Strasser and David Wolf.

The vision of the essay collection was developed in conversation with my agent, Karolina Sutton at Curtis Brown. As ever, I'm very grateful for her tireless support and enthusiasm for my writing.

I was delighted that this book gave me the chance to work again with Leo Hollis at Verso, who provides such calm yet sharp editorial judgement. I hope he's pleased with how it's turned out.

The turbulent period covered by this book coincided with another joyful, exhilarating, exhausting four years of family life. Thanks to Lydia, Martha and Laurie for making it endlessly fun and surprising, and for the pride they take in my writing.

The book is dedicated to my mum, and to the promise of normal times ahead.

Notes

Introduction

1   P. Norris and R. Inglehart, *Cultural Backlash: Trump, Brexit and Author-itarian Populism*, Cambridge University Press, 2018.

2   'Most Conservative members would see party destroyed to achieve Brexit', YouGov, 18 June 2019.

3   J. Dean, 'Communism or Neo-Feudalism?', *New Political Science* 42, 2020.

4   'The Times's endorsement for the general election: back to the future', *The Times*, 11 December 2019.

5   See N. Srnicek, *Platform Capitalism*, Polity, 2016.

6   T. Fetzer, 'Did Austerity Cause Brexit? Centre for Competitive Advantage in the Global Economy', University of Warwick, Working Paper No. 381, 2018.

7   See A. Tooze, *Crashed: How a Decade of Financial Crises Changed the World*, Allen Lane, 2018.

8   K. Milburn, *Generation Left*, Polity, 2019.

9   This is often referred to as 'economic imperialism'. See B. Fine and D. Milonakis, *From Economics Imperialism to Freakonomics: The Shifting Boundaries Between Economics and Other Social Sciences*, Routledge, 2009.

10   See N. Maclean, *Democracy in Chains: The Deep History of the Radical Right's Stealth Plan for America*, Penguin, 2016.

11   W. Davies, *The Limits of Neoliberalism: Authority, Sovereignty and the Logic of Competition*, Sage, 2014.

12   S. Zuboff, *The Age of Surveillance Capitalism: The Fight for a Human Future at the New Frontier of Power*, Profile Books, 2019.

13   See J. Vogl, *The Ascendency of Finance*, John Wiley, 2017.

14   See W. Streeck, *How Will Capitalism End? Essays on a Failing System*, Verso, 2017.

15   D. Harvey, 'The "New" Imperialism: Accumulation by Dispossession', *Socialist Register* 40.

16   As Jean-François Lyotard wrote in his 1979 *The Postmodern Condition* (Manchester University Press, 1984, pp. 4–5): 'The relationships of the suppliers and users of knowledge to the knowledge they supply and use is now tending, and will increasingly tend, to assume the form already taken by the relationship of commodity producers and consumers to the commodities they produce and consume – that is, the form of value. Knowledge is and will be produced in order to be sold, it is and will be consumed in order to be valorised in a new production: in both cases, the goal is exchange. Knowledge ceases to be an end in itself, it loses its "use-value".'

17   See P. Mair, *Ruling the Void: The Hollowing of Western Democracy*, Verso, 2013.

18   M. Feher, *Rated Agency: Investee Politics in a Speculative Age*, MIT Press, 2018.

19   See J. Meyer, 'The Making of the Fox News White House', *New Yorker*, 11 March 2019.

20   See M. Feher, 'The Political Ascendency of Creditworthiness', publicbooks.org, 1 September 2019; M. Feher, 'Disposing of the Discredited: A European Project', in W. Callison and Z. Manfredi (eds), *Mutant Neoliberalism: Market Rule and Political Rupture*, Fordham University Press, 2019.

21   The idea of 'real-time social science' was pioneered by Craig Calhoun, initially in response to the September 11 attacks.

1 'The People Have Spoken'

1 N. Fraser, 'Rethinking Recognition', *New Left Review*, May–June 2000.
2 J. Guo, 'What Donald Trump and Dying White People Have in Common', *Washington Post*, 15 December 2015.
3 M. Poovey, *A History of the Modern Fact*, University of Chicago Press, 1998.
4 G. Arrighi, *The Long Twentieth Century: Money, Power and the Origins of Our Time*, Verso, 2009.
5 See W. Streeck, *Buying Time: The Delayed Crisis of Democratic Capitalism*, Verso, 2014.
6 T. Piketty, *Capital in the Twenty-First Century*, Harvard University Press, 2014.
7 'Consultants reap rewards of Whitehall's Brexit scramble', *Financial Times*, 7 June 2019.
8 'Tony Blair admits he is baffled by rise of Bernie Sanders and Jeremy Corbyn', *Guardian*, 23 February 2016.
9 Esther Addley, 'Study shows 60% of Britons believe in conspiracy theories', *Guardian*, 23 November 2018.
10 B. Anderson, *Imagined Communities: Reflections on the Origin and Spread of Nationalism*, Verso, 2006.
11 H. Jones et al., *Go Home: The Politics of Immigration Controversies*, Manchester University Press, 2017.
12 H. Steward and P. Walker, 'Theresa May declares war on Brussels, urging: "Let me fight for Britain"', *Guardian*, 3 May 2017.

2 Quagmire

1 M. Fisher, *Ghosts of My Life*, Zero Books, 2014, p. 9.
2 D. Edgerton, *Britain's War Machine: Weapons, Resources, and Experts in the Second World War*, Oxford University Press, 2011.
3 Cabinet Office, 'The Future Relationship Between the United Kingdom and the European Union', 2018.
4 H. Arendt, *On Violence*, Houghton Mifflin Harcourt, 1970, p. 66.
5 'Donald Trump told Theresa May how to do Brexit "but she wrecked it" – and says the US trade deal is off', *Sun*, 13 July 2018.

6   B. Latour, *Down to Earth: Politics in the New Climatic Regime*, Polity, 2018, p. 2.

7   Ibid., p. 3.

8   A. Hirschman, *Exit, Voice, and Loyalty: Responses to Decline in Firms, Organizations, and States*, Harvard University Press, 1970, p. 43.

9   See Mair, *Ruling the Void*.

10   O. Hahl et al., 'The Authentic Appeal of the Lying Demagogue: Proclaiming the Deeper Truth about Political Illegitimacy', *American Sociological Review* 83:1, 2018.

11   S. Žižek, 'How Wikileaks opened our eyes to the illusion of freedom', *Guardian*, 19 June 2014.

12   'Police still not investigating Leave campaigns, citing "political sensitivities"', opendemocracy.net, 11 October 2018.

13   R. Seymour, 'The Economy of Reaction', patreon.com, 23 December 2018.

14   Anderson, *Imagined Communities*.

15   'Unhappiness with politics "at 15-year high"', BBC News, 8 April 2019.

3 'The People' Versus 'Politics'

1   P. Gerbaudo, *The Digital Party: Political Organisation and Online Democracy*, Pluto, 2018.

2   Ibid., p. xx.

3   T. Bale, 'Tory leadership: who gets to choose the UK's next prime minister?', BBC News, 23 June 2019.

4   'Most Conservative members would see party destroyed', YouGov.

5   'Everything you think you know about Leavers and Remainers is wrong', Britain in a Changing Europe, 11 June 2019.

6   'Johnson pledges to make all immigrants learn English', *Guardian*, 5 July 2019.

7   T. Veblen, *Theory of the Leisure Class*, Random House, 2001.

8   H. Arendt, 'Truth and Politics', in *Between Past and Future: Eight Exercises in Political Thought*, Penguin, 1993, p. 250.

9   'Majority worldwide say their society is broken – an increasing feeling among Britons', Ipsos Mori, 13 September 2019.

10　Y. Benkler et al., *Network Propaganda: Manipulation, Disinformation, and Radicalization in American Politics*, Oxford University Press, 2018.

11　G. Blank, 'The Myth of the Echo Chamber', OII blog, 9 March 2018.

12　Ipsos.com, 'Ipsos MORI Veracity Index 2019: Trust in Professions Survey', November 2019.

13　M. Andrejevic, '"Framelessness" or the Cultural Logic of Big Data', in M. S. Daubs and V. R. Manzerolle (eds), *Mobile and Ubiquitous Media: Critical and International Perspectives*, Peter Lang, 2014.

14　P. Ford, 'The Web is a Customer Service Medium', Ftrain.com, 6 January 2011.

15　M. Weber, 'Politics as a Vocation', in *From Max Weber: Essays in Sociology*, Routledge, 1991, p. 116.

16　'Tories pretend to be factchecking service during leaders' debate', *Guardian*, 19 November 2019.

Afterword: In the Wreckage of Liberalism

1　'Trust in UK government and news media COVID-19 information down, concerns over misinformation from government and politicians up', Reuters Institute, 1 June 2020.

2　'Brits see cleaner air, stronger social bonds and changing food habits amid lockdown', RSA, 17 April 2020.

3　R. Hendrikse, 'Neo-illiberalism', *Geoforum*, 95, 2018.

4　K. Pistor, *The Code of Capital: How the Law Creates Wealth and Inequality*, Princeton University Press, 2019.

5　See W. Callison and Z. Manfredi (eds), *Mutant Neoliberalism*, Fordham University Press, 2019.

6　On the patrimonial quality of Trumpism, see D. Riley, 'What is Trump?', *New Left Review* 114, November–December 2018.